The Australian Women's Weekly cookbooks

Food editor *Pamela Clark*
Assistant food editors *Jan Castorina, Karen Green*
Associate food editor *Enid Morrison*
Chief home economist *Kathy Wharton*
Deputy chief home economist *Louise Patniotis*
Home economists *Tracey Kern, Quinton Kohler,
Jill Lange, Alexandra McCowan, Kathy McGarry,
Kathy Snowball, Dimitra Stais*
Editorial coordinator *Elizabeth Hooper*
Kitchen assistant *Amy Wong*

Designers *Louise McGeachie, Paula Wooller*
Stylists *Marie-Helene Clauzon, Rosemary de Santis,
Carolyn Fienberg, Jacqui Hing, Kathy Wharton*
Photographers *Kevin Brown, Robert Clark,
Robert Taylor, Jon Waddy*

Home Library Staff
Editor-in-chief *Mary Coleman*
Marketing manager *Nicole Pizanis*
Designers *Sue de Guingand, Caryl Wiggins,
Alison Windmill, Michele Withers*
Studio manager/ designer *Caryl Wiggins*
Subeditor *Bianca Martin*
Editorial coordinators *Fiona Lambrou, Kate Neil*

Managing director *Colin Morrison*
Group publisher *Paul Dykzeul*

Produced by *The Australian Women's Weekly*
Home Library, Sydney.
Colour separations by ACP Colour Graphics Pty Ltd.
Printing by Times Printers Pte Limited, Singapore.
Published by ACP Publishing Pty Limited,
54 Park St, Sydney; GPO Box 4088, Sydney, NSW 1028.
Ph: (02) 9282 8618 Fax: (02) 9267 9438.
AWWHomeLib@publishing.acp.com.au

AUSTRALIA: Distributed by Network Distribution
Company, GPO Box 4088, Sydney, NSW 1028.
Ph: (02) 9282 8777 Fax: (02) 9264 3278.
UNITED KINGDOM: Distributed in the UK by
Australian Consolidated Press (UK),
Moulton Park Business Centre, Red House Rd,
Moulton Park, Northhampton, NN3 6AQ,
Ph: (01604) 497531 Fax: (01604) 497 533
Acpukltd@aol.com
CANADA: Distributed in Canada by
Whitecap Books Ltd, 351 Lynn Ave, North Vancouver,
BC, V7J 2C4, (604) 980 9852.
NEW ZEALAND: Distributed in New Zealand by
Netlink Distribution Company, 17B Hargreaves St,
Level 5, College Hill, Auckland 1, (9) 302 7616.
SOUTH AFRICA: Distributed in South Africa by
PSD Promotions (Pty) Ltd, PO Box 1175,
Isando 1600, SA, (011) 392 6065

Pasta Cookbook
Includes index.
ISBN 0 949128 35 X
1. Cookery. (Pasta). (Series: Australian Women's
Weekly Home Library).
641.882

ACP Publishing Pty Limited 1999
ACN 053 273 546

Cover: Creamy Lemon Zucchini Pasta Sauce, page 100.
Back cover: from back: Spicy Tortellini Salad;
Creamy Bacon and Basil Tagliatelle, page 92.

KT-386-423

Pasta cookbook

Pasta and noodles fascinate us; their shapes are so varied and the number of ways to use them is almost endless! The name of the pasta, often Italian, describes its shape or type: for example, spaghetti means "little strings". Names often vary, so choose pasta by shape if you can't find what we specify. Where we specify fresh pasta dough, you can easily make this by following our step-by-step guide on pages 120-122. Filled pasta, such as ravioli and tortellini, are bought unless we specify how to make your own. The noodles we used are mostly of oriental origin. Also, see the glossary for information.

Pamela Clark
FOOD EDITOR

1 tagliatelle all 'uovo 2 bucatini 3 penne rigate 4 bavette 5 paglia e fieno
6 wholemeal spaghetti 7 lasagne 8 rigatoni 9 tagliatelle 10 lasagnette 11 fusilli
12 conchigliette 13 fusilli bucati lunghi 14 pipe rigati 15 ziti 16 ditalini rigati 17 filini
18 gnocchi 19 tortiglioni 20 stelline 21 farfalle 22 casarecce 23 lasagne verdi
24 spaghettini 25 cannelloni 26 maccheroni 27 farfalline 28 risoni 29 penne lisce

BRITISH & NORTH AMERICAN READERS:
Please note that Australian cup and spoon
measurements are metric. A quick conversion
guide appears on page 128.
A glossary explaining unfamiliar terms and
ingredients appears on page 122.

SOUPS & ENTREES

You will enjoy the fresh, light and pretty look of our marvellous entrees, though some, of course, have to be classed as hearty eating! Some are hot, some cold, and some between, such as a warm pasta salad. There are lovely sauces, too, and soups, including our version of minestrone. If you prefer, serve these recipes as lunches, snacks or main meals. However, for good menu balance, the main course should not contain pasta if you serve it in a soup or entree.

SPINACH AND CABANOSSI PARCELS WITH PASTA

1 bunch (40 leaves) English spinach
2 tablespoons olive oil
2 cloves garlic, crushed
1 carrot, grated
2 small zucchini, grated
1 stick (125g) cabanossi, finely chopped
3 green shallots, chopped
125g ricotta cheese
¼ teaspoon ground nutmeg
300g fettucine pasta

TOMATO SAUCE
2 x 425g cans tomatoes
2 onions, chopped
2 teaspoons dried oregano leaves
2 tablespoons tomato paste
2 teaspoons sugar

Add spinach to pan of boiling water, drain immediately, rinse under cold water; drain, press out as much water as possible.

Heat oil in pan, add garlic, carrot and zucchini, cook, stirring, until vegetables are soft; cool. Combine vegetable mixture, cabanossi, shallots, cheese and nutmeg in bowl; mix well.

Place a level tablespoon of mixture on centre of 2 overlapping spinach leaves, fold in sides and roll up firmly. Repeat with remaining mixture and spinach.

Just before serving, add pasta to large pan of boiling water, boil, uncovered, until just tender; drain. Place parcels in single layer in top half of steamer, cook over boiling water for about 2 minutes or until heated through. Serve parcels with pasta and warm sauce.

Tomato Sauce: Combine undrained crushed tomatoes with remaining ingredients in pan. Bring to boil, boil, uncovered, for about 10 minutes or until slightly thickened. Blend or process sauce for 10 seconds.

Makes about 20.

■ Parcels and sauce can be made a day ahead.
■ Storage: Covered, in refrigerator.
■ Freeze: Sauce suitable.
■ Microwave: Suitable.

PRAWN AND NOODLE BUNDLES

12 (about 500g) uncooked king prawns
200g Japanese somen noodles
¾ cup cornflour
2 teaspoons sake
2 egg yolks
2 tablespoons water, approximately
12 chives
oil for deep-frying

WASABI SOY SAUCE
2 tablespoons light soy sauce
2 teaspoons sake
2 teaspoons sugar
¼ teaspoon wasabi paste

Shell and devein prawns, leaving tails intact. Break noodles in half.

Blend sifted cornflour with sake, egg yolks and enough water to mix to a smooth batter. Dip each prawn in batter, roll in noodles; cover, refrigerate 1 hour or until noodles cling to batter.

Add chives to pan of boiling water, drain immediately, rinse under cold water; drain.

Just before serving, deep-fry bundles in hot oil until lightly browned and cooked through; drain on absorbent paper. Tie each prawn bundle with a chive; serve hot prawns with sauce.

Wasabi Soy Sauce: Combine all ingredients in bowl, stir until sugar is dissolved.

Makes 12.

■ Prawns and sauce can be prepared a day ahead.
■ Storage: Separately, covered, in refrigerator.
■ Freeze: Not suitable.
■ Microwave: Not suitable.

RIGHT: From front: Prawn and Noodle Bundles, Spinach and Cabanossi Parcels with Pasta.

Plates from Butler & Co.

SPICY PUMPKIN SOUP WITH BEEF TORTELLINI

250g beef tortellini
2 tablespoons olive oil
1 onion, chopped
1 clove garlic, crushed
½ teaspoon ground coriander
1 teaspoon ground cumin
1 teaspoon cracked black
   peppercorns
1kg pumpkin, chopped
1 potato, chopped
1 litre (4 cups) water
1 small chicken stock cube, crumbled
½ cup cream
1 tablespoon chopped fresh chives
1 tablespoon chopped fresh basil

Add tortellini to large pan of boiling water, boil, uncovered, until just tender; drain.

Heat oil in pan, add onion, garlic, coriander and cumin, cook, stirring, until onion is soft. Stir in peppercorns, pumpkin and potato, cook, stirring, for 2 minutes. Stir in water and stock cube, bring to boil, simmer, covered, for 15 minutes or until vegetables are soft; cool slightly. Blend or process mixture in batches until smooth. **Just before serving,** return soup to pan, stir in cream, herbs and tortellini, stir over heat until heated through.

Serves 6.

■ Can be prepared a day ahead.
■ Storage: Covered, in refrigerator.
■ Freeze: Not suitable.
■ Microwave: Not suitable.

QUICK 'N' EASY CHICKEN SOUP

40g butter
¼ cup plain flour
3 small chicken stock cubes,
   crumbled
3 cups hot water
½ cup crushed rice vermicelli
1 cup (200g) finely chopped
   cooked chicken
2 tablespoons lemon juice
1 teaspoon dried tarragon leaves

Heat butter in pan, add flour, cook, stirring, until bubbling. Remove from heat, gradually stir in stock cubes and water. Stir over heat until mixture boils and thickens. Add vermicelli, chicken, juice and tarragon, stir until heated through.

Serves 4.

■ Soup can be made a day ahead.
■ Storage: Covered, in refrigerator.
■ Freeze: Suitable.
■ Microwave: Suitable.

LAMB SHANK AND CELERY SOUP

2 tablespoons olive oil
2 cloves garlic, crushed
3 lamb shanks
1½ litres (6 cups) water
1 cup dry red wine
1 tablespoon olive oil, extra
1 onion, chopped
1 cup (100g) pasta elbows
4 sticks celery, chopped
2 tablespoons chopped fresh parsley

Heat oil in large pan, add garlic and shanks, cook until shanks are well browned all over. Add water and wine, bring to boil, simmer, uncovered, for about 1 hour or until lamb is tender.

Strain, reserve stock; remove lamb from bones, shred lamb finely. Heat extra oil in same pan, add onion, cook, stirring, until soft. Add reserved stock, bring to boil, add pasta, boil, uncovered, until pasta is almost tender. Stir in celery and lamb, simmer further 10 minutes. Add parsley just before serving.

Serves 6.

■ Soup can be made a day ahead.
■ Storage: Covered, in refrigerator.
■ Freeze: Suitable.
■ Microwave: Suitable.

LEFT: Clockwise from top: Spicy Pumpkin Soup with Beef Tortellini, Lamb Shank and Celery Soup, Quick 'n' Easy Chicken Soup.

CHILLI WONTON SOUP

1 carrot
1½ litres (6 cups) water
2 sticks celery, chopped
2 small beef stock cubes, crumbled
½ teaspoon grated fresh ginger
3 green shallots, chopped

WONTONS
30g butter
1 onion, finely chopped
2 teaspoons plain flour
125g pork and veal mince
2 mushrooms, finely chopped
1 tablespoon tomato paste
1 teaspoon Worcestershire sauce
¼ teaspoon chilli powder
36 x 8cm square wonton wrappers

Cut carrot into thin strips. Combine carrot, water, celery, stock cubes, ginger and shallots in pan, bring to boil, boil, uncovered, for 5 minutes. Add wontons, cook 1 minute before serving.

Wontons: Heat butter in pan, add onion, cook, stirring, until soft. Combine onion, flour, mince, mushrooms, paste, sauce and chilli in bowl; mix well.

Place 1 heaped teaspoon of mixture on centre of each wonton wrapper. Brush

edges of wrappers lightly with water, gather edges around filling, pinch together firmly.

Add wontons to pan of boiling water, boil, uncovered, until wontons float to surface, simmer 10 minutes; drain.

Makes 36.

■ Wontons can be prepared a day ahead. Soup base can be made a day ahead.
■ Storage: Covered, in refrigerator.
■ Freeze: Uncooked wontons suitable.
■ Microwave: Soup base suitable.

PRAWN AND NOODLE SALAD WITH HONEY DRESSING

250g fine fresh egg noodles
2 sticks celery, chopped
1 large carrot, chopped
1 large onion, chopped
125g snow peas
500g cooked prawns, shelled

HONEY DRESSING
½ cup light soy sauce
½ cup water
2 tablespoons honey
2 tablespoons chopped fresh
**   coriander**
1 clove garlic, crushed

Add noodles to large pan of boiling water, boil, uncovered, until just tender, drain; rinse under cold water, drain.

Cut noodles in half. Boil, steam or microwave vegetables until just tender, rinse under cold water, drain.

Just before serving, combine noodles, vegetables and prawns in bowl; top with dressing.

Honey Dressing: Combine all ingredients in jar; shake well.

Serves 6.

■ Can be prepared a day ahead.
■ Storage: Covered, in refrigerator.
■ Freeze: Not suitable.
■ Microwave: Suitable.

CREAMED MUSHROOM AND PASTRAMI PASTA

500g fusilli pasta
20g butter
1 tablespoon olive oil
2 cloves garlic, crushed
4 green shallots, sliced
1 small red pepper, sliced
200g baby mushrooms, halved
1 small chicken stock cube, crumbled
2 teaspoons cornflour
1 cup water
½ cup dry white wine
¼ teaspoon dried marjoram leaves
125g sliced pastrami, sliced
½ cup thickened cream

Add pasta to large pan of boiling water, boil, uncovered, until just tender; drain.

Heat butter and oil in pan, add garlic, cook, stirring, 1 minute. Add shallots,

pepper and mushrooms, stir over heat for 2 minutes. Blend stock cube and cornflour with 2 tablespoons of the water in bowl, stir in remaining water, wine and marjoram. Stir cornflour mixture into vegetable mixture, stir until sauce boils and thickens.

Just before serving, combine warm sauce, pastrami, cream and noodles in pan, stir until heated through.

Serves 4.

■ Can be prepared 6 hours ahead.
■ Storage: Covered, at room temperature.
■ Freeze: Not suitable.
■ Microwave: Suitable.

ANGEL PASTA WITH CREAMY SALMON AND CAVIAR

250g capelli d'angelo pasta
100g smoked salmon pieces
300ml carton thickened cream
2 tablespoons chopped red
**   Spanish onion**
1 tablespoon chopped fresh chives
50g salmon roe (caviar)

Add pasta to large pan of boiling water, boil, uncovered, until just tender, drain; keep warm.

Cut salmon into strips. Heat cream in pan, bring to boil, simmer, add onion, cook until heated through. Stir in chives, remove from heat, add salmon and roe. Stir gently to separate roe. Serve sauce over pasta.

Serves 4.

■ Best made close to serving.
■ Freeze: Not suitable.
■ Microwave: Pasta suitable.

LEFT: Clockwise from left: Chilli Wonton Soup, Creamed Mushroom and Pastrami Pasta, Prawn and Noodle Salad with Honey Dressing.
ABOVE: Angel Pasta with Creamy Salmon and Caviar.

Left: Plates and bowls from Villa Italiana

SESAME ROAST DUCK WITH HERBED PASTA

1 quantity herbed pasta dough
1 Chinese roast duck
310g can mandarin segments, drained
½ x 160g punnet snow pea sprouts

SESAME DRESSING
⅓ cup olive oil
1 tablespoon sesame oil
¼ teaspoon five spice powder
1 clove garlic, crushed
⅓ cup lime juice
2 tablespoons honey
1 teaspoon sesame seeds

Roll dough until 2mm thick, cut into 8 x 12cm squares. Add pasta to large pan of boiling water, boil, uncovered, until just tender, drain, rinse under hot water; drain.

Remove meat from duck, cut meat into 1cm slices. Combine duck meat, mandarins and sprouts in bowl.

Just before serving, place a square of pasta onto each plate. Divide half the duck mixture over squares, sprinkle with a little of the dressing; repeat layering.
Sesame Dressing: Combine all ingredients in jar; shake well.
Serves 4.

■ Can be prepared 6 hours ahead.
■ Storage: Covered, in refrigerator.
■ Freeze: Not suitable.
■ Microwave: Pasta suitable.

BELOW: Sesame Roast Duck with Herbed Pasta.
RIGHT: From left: Chicken Wing Pockets with Tasty Risoni Filling, Minestrone.

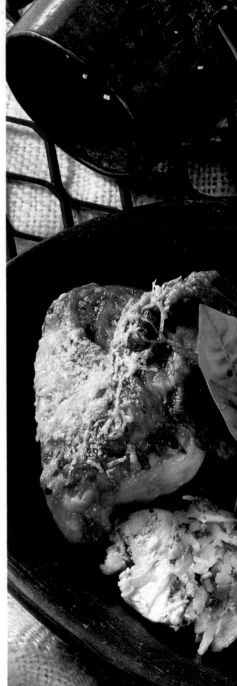

MINESTRONE

2 tablespoons olive oil
1kg veal bones
3 litres (12 cups) water
4 ripe tomatoes, peeled, chopped
1½ cups (200g) small macaroni pasta
2 carrots, chopped
1 leek, thinly sliced
2 zucchini, sliced
440g can red kidney beans, rinsed, drained
2 tablespoons tomato paste
½ teaspoon sugar
3 English spinach leaves, shredded
¼ cup chopped fresh parsley

Heat oil in large heavy-based saucepan, add bones, cook, stirring, until well browned all over. Add water, bring to boil, simmer, covered, for 1 hour. Remove and discard bones from stock.

Bring stock to boil, stir in tomatoes and macaroni, simmer, uncovered, for 10 minutes. Stir in carrots, leek, zucchini, beans, paste and sugar. Bring to boil, simmer, uncovered, for about 10 minutes or until leek is tender. Stir in spinach and parsley just before serving.

Serves 8.

■ Recipe can be made a day ahead.
■ Storage: Covered, in refrigerator.
■ Freeze: Not suitable.
■ Microwave: Not suitable.

CHICKEN WING POCKETS WITH TASTY RISONI FILLING

8 large chicken wings
⅓ cup risoni pasta
2 tablespoons chopped fresh basil
1 tablespoon chopped fresh chives
50g chopped salami
2 tablespoons chopped black olives
½ teaspoon cracked black
   peppercorns
1 tablespoon tomato paste
1 teaspoon olive oil
30g butter, melted
⅓ cup grated fresh
   parmesan cheese

Holding large end of third joint of chicken wing, trim around bone with knife. Cut, scrape and push meat down to second joint, without cutting skin. Twist bone and remove; discard bone.

Add pasta to large pan of boiling water, boil, uncovered, until just tender; drain. Combine pasta, herbs, salami, olives, peppercorns, paste and oil in bowl. Spoon mixture into chicken wing cavities, secure openings with toothpicks.

Just before serving, brush wings with butter, place on rack over baking dish. Bake in a moderate oven for 30 minutes, sprinkle with cheese, bake further 10 minutes or until chicken is tender.

Makes 8.

■ Can be prepared a day ahead.
■ Storage: Covered, in refrigerator.
■ Freeze: Uncooked wings suitable.
■ Microwave: Not suitable.

SCALLOP RAVIOLI WITH LOBSTER BASIL SAUCE

1 quantity plain pasta dough

SCALLOP FILLING
300g scallops
1 egg white
2 tablespoons grated parmesan cheese
¼ cup cream

LOBSTER BASIL SAUCE
1 medium lobster tail
30g butter
1 onion, finely chopped
1 clove garlic, crushed
300ml carton cream
¼ cup dry white wine
1½ teaspoons cornflour
1 tablespoon water
2 tablespoons shredded fresh basil leaves

Roll pasta dough until 2mm thick, cut into 24 x 8cm rounds. Spoon filling evenly onto centres of half the rounds, leaving a 5mm border around edges. Brush edges lightly with water, top with remaining rounds, pinch edges firmly together to seal.

Just before serving, add ravioli to large pan of boiling water, boil, uncovered, for about 3 minutes or until tender; drain. Serve ravioli with sauce.

Scallop Filling: Remove roe and trim scallops. Blend or process scallops, egg white and cheese until smooth. Add cream, process until just combined.

Lobster Basil Sauce: Remove meat from lobster tail, chop meat finely. Heat butter in pan, add onion and garlic, cook, stirring, until onion is soft. Add meat, cook,

stirring, for 1 minute. Stir in cream and wine, then blended cornflour and water, stir over heat until sauce boils and thickens; stir in basil.

Serves 4 to 6.

■ Ravioli and sauce can be made a day ahead.
■ Storage: Covered, in refrigerator.
■ Freeze: Uncooked ravioli suitable.
■ Microwave: Not suitable.

HERBED BEEF PARCELS WITH RED PEPPER SAUCE

¼ quantity plain pasta dough
1 tablespoon olive oil
1 small onion, chopped
2 cloves garlic, crushed
500g minced beef
⅓ cup dry red wine
½ cup sour cream
¼ cup grated gruyere cheese
1 tablespoon chopped fresh parsley
1 tablespoon chopped fresh basil
1 tablespoon chopped fresh chives
1 tablespoon tomato paste
1 small beef stock cube, crumbled
1 tablespoon sour cream, extra
1 tablespoon thickened cream
2 teaspoons chopped fresh
    chives, extra
2 tablespoons grated gruyere
    cheese, extra

RED PEPPER SAUCE
2 red peppers
410g can tomatoes
¼ cup cream
¼ teaspoon sugar

Roll pasta dough until 2mm thick, cut into 4 x 12cm squares. Add squares to large pan of boiling water, boil, uncovered, until just tender; drain.

Heat oil in pan, add onion and garlic, cook, stirring, until onion is soft. Add beef, cook, stirring, until well browned. Stir in wine, sour cream, cheese, herbs, paste and stock cube. Bring to boil, simmer, uncovered, for about 10 minutes or until thickened.

Place quarter of the meat mixture on centre of each pasta square, pinch corners together. Spoon sauce onto plates, pipe with combined extra sour cream and thickened cream, top with parcel, then extra chives and extra cheese.
Red Pepper Sauce: Quarter peppers, remove seeds and membrane. Grill peppers, skin side up, until skin blackens and blisters; peel skin. Blend or process peppers, undrained tomatoes, cream and sugar until smooth.

Serves 4.

■ Recipe best made just before serving.
■ Freeze: Not suitable.
■ Microwave: Pasta suitable.

CHEESE TORTELLINI LOAF WITH TOMATO SALSA

500g cheese tortellini
4 eggs, lightly beaten
300ml carton thickened cream
1 cup (80g) grated fresh
    parmesan cheese

TOMATO SALSA
3 ripe tomatoes, peeled, chopped
4 green shallots, chopped
2 tablespoons chopped fresh basil
½ teaspoon sugar

Lightly grease 14cm x 21cm loaf pan, line base with paper, grease paper. Add tortellini to large pan of boiling water, boil, uncovered, until just tender; drain.

Combine eggs, cream and cheese in bowl, beat until just combined. Stir in tortellini, pour mixture into prepared pan. Place pan in baking dish, pour enough boiling water into dish to come halfway up sides of pan. Bake, uncovered, in moderate oven for about 45 minutes or until set. Serve warm with tomato salsa.

Tomato Salsa: Combine all ingredients in bowl; mix well.

Serves 6.

■ Recipe can be made a day ahead.
■ Storage: Covered, in refrigerator.
■ Freeze: Not suitable.
■ Microwave: Not suitable.

ABOVE LEFT: From left: Herbed Beef Parcels with Red Pepper Sauce, Scallop Ravioli with Lobster Basil Sauce.
ABOVE: Cheese Tortellini Loaf with Tomato Salsa.

Above: China from Villeroy & Boch

NUTTY CHICKEN AND PASTA LOAF WITH EGG SURPRISES

½ cup risoni pasta
500g chicken thigh fillets
1 clove garlic, crushed
1 onion, chopped
2 tablespoons tomato paste
1 teaspoon dried marjoram leaves
1 small chicken stock cube, crumbled
1 zucchini, finely chopped
⅓ cup pine nuts, toasted
4 hard-boiled eggs
½ bunch (20 leaves) English spinach

CHUTNEY MAYONNAISE
½ cup mayonnaise
¼ cup cream
¼ cup mango chutney
1 tablespoon chopped fresh mint

Line base and sides of 11cm x 21cm ovenproof loaf dish with plastic wrap. Add pasta to pan of boiling water, boil, uncovered, until just tender; drain, cool.

Blend or process chicken, garlic, onion, paste, marjoram and stock cube until smooth; transfer mixture to bowl. Combine chicken mixture with pasta, zucchini, nuts and 1 chopped egg; mix well.

Add spinach to pan of boiling water, drain immediately, rinse under cold water; drain, pat dry with absorbent paper.

Line base and sides of prepared dish with three-quarters of the spinach leaves. Press half the chicken mixture evenly over base of dish, place remaining eggs along centre, cover with remaining chicken mixture, pressing down firmly, smooth surface. Top with remaining spinach. Cover dish with plastic wrap, then foil.

Place dish in baking dish, pour in enough boiling water to come halfway up sides of dish. Bake in moderate oven for 1 hour. Stand loaf 5 minutes before turning out. Serve loaf warm or cold with chutney mayonnaise.

Chutney Mayonnaise: Blend or process mayonnaise, cream and chutney until smooth; stir in mint.

Serves 6.

- Recipe can be prepared or made a day ahead.
- Storage: Covered, in refrigerator.
- Freeze: Not suitable.
- Microwave: Spinach suitable.

SALAD OF PASTA PILLOWS WITH BALSAMIC VINAIGRETTE

1 quantity plain pasta dough
1 bunch curly endive
1 mignonette lettuce
250g punnet cherry tomatoes

TURKEY AND NUT FILLING
2 teaspoons olive oil
1 small onion, chopped
¼ bunch (10 leaves) English spinach, chopped
300g sliced turkey breast roll, chopped
⅓ cup pine nuts, toasted
1 tablespoon grated parmesan cheese
2 tablespoons cottage cheese

BALSAMIC VINAIGRETTE
½ cup olive oil
2 tablespoons balsamic vinegar
2 teaspoons lemon juice
1 clove garlic, crushed
2 teaspoons chopped fresh basil

Roll pasta dough until 2mm thick, cut 6cm rounds from pasta. Top each round with 1 level teaspoon of filling, brush edges lightly with water, fold rounds in half, press edges together firmly.

Just before serving, add pasta pillows to large pan of boiling water, boil, uncovered, for about 4 minutes or until tender; drain, cool.

Place endive, lettuce, pasta pillows and tomatoes on plate, pour over vinaigrette.

Turkey and Nut Filling: Heat oil in pan, add onion, cook, stirring, until soft. Blend or process spinach until fine, add onion mixture, turkey, nuts and cheeses, blend or process until fine.

Balsamic Vinaigrette: Combine all ingredients in jar; shake well.

Serves 6.

- Pasta pillows can be prepared 6 hours ahead. Vinaigrette can be made 2 days ahead.
- Storage: Covered, in refrigerator.
- Freeze: Uncooked pasta pillows suitable.
- Microwave: Not suitable.

HERBED FISH AND PASTA SOUP

20g butter
1 leek, thinly sliced
1 carrot, chopped
1 teaspoon chopped fresh thyme
300g white fish fillets, chopped
100g capelli d'angelo pasta

FISH STOCK
500g fish bones
1½ litres (6 cups) water

Heat butter in pan, add leek and carrot, cook, stirring, until leek is soft. Add thyme and 5 cups of the fish stock, bring to boil, simmer, uncovered, for about 15 minutes or until carrot is soft. Add fish and pasta, bring to boil, boil, uncovered, for about 10 minutes or until pasta is tender.

Fish Stock: Combine fish bones and water in large pan, Bring to boil, simmer, uncovered, for 20 minutes; strain.
Serves 4.

■ Soup can be made a day ahead.
■ Storage: Covered, in refrigerator.
■ Freeze: Fish stock suitable.
■ Microwave: Soup suitable.

ABOVE: From left: Nutty Chicken and Pasta Loaf with Egg Surprises, Herbed Fish and Pasta Soup, Salad of Pasta Pillows with Balsamic Vinaigrette.

Plates from Corso de Fiori; spoons from Home and Garden

STEAK STRIPS WITH TOMATO TAGLIATELLE

375g piece rump steak
200g broccoli, chopped
2 tablespoons chopped
   fresh coriander
2 tablespoons chopped fresh parsley
1 clove garlic, crushed
12 thick slices bread
40g butter, melted
1 tablespoon olive oil
375g tomato tagliatelle pasta
2 tablespoons olive oil, extra
1 onion, thinly sliced

FRUITY YOGURT SAUCE
1 egg
1 tablespoon chutney
1 teaspoon grated lemon rind
2 tablespoons lemon juice
¼ cup plain yogurt
1 tablespoon finely chopped
   fresh mint

Cut excess fat from steak, cut steak into thin strips. Combine steak, broccoli, herbs and garlic in bowl, mix well; cover, refrigerate 1 hour.

Cut an 8cm round from each slice of bread, brush both sides of rounds with combined butter and oil. Place rounds onto oven tray, bake in moderate oven for about 15 minutes or until well browned.

Just before serving, add pasta to large pan of boiling water, boil, uncovered, until just tender; drain.

Heat extra oil in pan, add onion, cook, stirring, until lightly browned. Add steak mixture, cook, stirring, until steak is well browned and tender. Combine steak mixture with pasta, serve on warm toast rounds with sauce.

Fruity Yogurt Sauce: Blend or process all ingredients until smooth.

Serves 6.

■ Steak can be prepared a day ahead. Toast can be made 3 days ahead.
■ Storage: Steak, covered, in refrigerator. Toast rounds, in airtight container.
■ Freeze: Toast rounds suitable.
■ Microwave: Pasta suitable.

BALMAIN BUG TORTELLINI WITH CURRY CREAM

10 cooked Balmain bugs
1 quantity plain pasta dough

CURRY CREAM
30g butter
3 teaspoons curry powder
2 green shallots, chopped
½ teaspoon ground cumin
1 small fresh red chilli, chopped
2 x 150g cans coconut milk
¼ cup water

Place Balmain bugs, back down, on board, cut tails from body using sharp knife. Cut through tail lengthways, remove vein; remove tail meat, chop meat finely.

Roll pasta dough until 2mm thick, cut 5cm rounds from dough. Cut rounds in half, top each half with a piece of Balmain bug meat, brush edges lightly with water. Fold rounds in half, press edges together.

Just before serving, add tortellini to large pan of boiling water, boil, uncovered, for about 3 minutes or until tortellini are tender; drain. Combine tortellini and hot curry cream in bowl.

Curry Cream: Heat butter in pan, add curry powder, shallots, cumin and chilli, cook, stirring, for 1 minute. Stir in coconut milk and water, bring to boil, simmer, uncovered, for about 5 minutes or until sauce thickens slightly.

Serves 4.

- Tortellini and curry cream can be made a day ahead.
- Storage: Covered, in refrigerator.
- Freeze: Uncooked tortellini suitable.
- Microwave: Not suitable.

CHILLI BEEF STIR-FRY IN NOODLE NESTS

375g rump steak, thinly sliced
1 teaspoon grated fresh ginger
2 tablespoons dry white wine
1 tablespoon olive oil
1 onion, chopped
1 red pepper, chopped
1 carrot, sliced
1 teaspoon cornflour
⅓ cup water
1 small chicken stock cube, crumbled
1 tablespoon sambal oelek
1 teaspoon sesame oil
1 teaspoon brown sugar
1 tablespoon tomato sauce
3 large leaves spinach (silverbeet), shredded

NOODLE NESTS
125g capellini egg noodles
2 egg yolks, lightly beaten

Combine steak, ginger and wine in bowl; cover, refrigerate 2 hours.

Heat oil in wok or pan, add steak mixture in batches, stir-fry until well browned; remove from wok.

Add onion, pepper and carrot to wok, stir-fry for 2 minutes. Return steak to wok, stir in blended cornflour and water, stock cube, sambal oelek, sesame oil, sugar and sauce. Stir until mixture boils and thickens slightly, remove from heat; stir in spinach.

Just before serving, spoon hot mixture into hot noodle nests.

Noodle Nests: Add noodles to large pan of boiling water, boil, uncovered, until just tender; drain well.

Combine hot noodles with egg yolks in bowl; mix well. Divide mixture between 6 x 10cm diameter greased pie tins, bringing noodles up the sides of tins. Place tins on oven tray, bake in hot oven for 30 minutes, gently remove nests from tins, place nests upside down on oven tray. Bake further 15 minutes or until bases are well browned and crisp.

Makes 6.

- Nests and filling can be prepared 6 hours ahead.
- Storage: Covered, in refrigerator.
- Freeze: Not suitable.
- Microwave: Not suitable.

CHEESE RAVIOLI WITH PECAN AND CORIANDER PESTO

1 quantity plain pasta dough

FILLING
200g feta cheese, mashed
100g ricotta cheese
½ teaspoon ground cinnamon

PECAN AND CORIANDER PESTO
⅓ cup chopped pecan nuts, toasted
1 tablespoon pine nuts, toasted
2 cloves garlic, chopped
½ cup chopped fresh coriander
¼ cup sour light cream
½ cup olive oil

Cut pasta dough into 4 portions, roll each portion until 2mm thick. Place ½ level teaspoons of filling 4cm apart over 2 pasta sheets. Lightly brush remaining sheets of pasta with water, place over filling, press firmly between filling. Cut into 4cm square ravioli shapes.

Just before serving, add ravioli to large pan of boiling water, boil, uncovered, for about 5 minutes or until tender; drain. Lightly toss hot ravioli with pecan and coriander pesto.

Filling: Combine cheeses and cinnamon in bowl; beat until smooth.

Pecan and Coriander Pesto: Blend or process all ingredients until combined.

Serves 6.

- Ravioli and pesto can be made a day ahead.
- Storage: Covered, in refrigerator.
- Freeze: Uncooked ravioli suitable.
- Microwave: Not suitable.

LEFT: From left: Steak Strips with Tomato Tagliatelle, Balmain Bug Tortellini with Curry Cream.
BELOW: From left: Cheese Ravioli with Pecan and Coriander Pesto, Chilli Beef Stir-Fry in Noodle Nests.
Below: China from Villeroy & Boch

WARM SALMON AND ASPARAGUS SALAD

We used Atlantic salmon.

375g piece salmon
1 bunch (12 spears) asparagus,
   chopped
30g butter
1 clove garlic, crushed
250g fettucine pasta
20g butter, melted, extra
2 tablespoons chopped fresh oregano

BASIL SAUCE
½ cup water
2 teaspoons French mustard
2 tablespoons dry white wine
1 tablespoon lemon juice
2½ teaspoons cornflour
1 tablespoon water, extra
½ cup thickened cream
2 tablespoons shredded fresh basil

Remove skin and bones from salmon, slice salmon thinly. Boil, steam or microwave asparagus until just tender; drain. Heat butter in pan, add garlic, cook, stirring, for 1 minute. Add salmon, cook, stirring gently, for about 2 minutes or until just cooked through, stir in asparagus.

Just before serving, add pasta to large pan of boiling water, boil, uncovered, until just tender; drain. Toss pasta with extra butter and oregano. Serve with warm asparagus, salmon mixture and sauce.

Basil Sauce: Combine water, mustard, wine and juice in pan, bring to boil. Stir in blended cornflour and extra water, stir until sauce boils and thickens slightly. Remove from heat, stir in cream and basil.

Serves 4.

■ Salmon mixture can be prepared 3 hours ahead.
■ Storage: Covered, in refrigerator.
■ Freeze: Not suitable.
■ Microwave: Pasta and sauce suitable.

BEEF AND PASTA SALAD WITH CREAMY HORSERADISH

500g piece beef eye-fillet
1 tablespoon olive oil
3 cups (200g) farfalle pasta
200g snow peas
1 red pepper, sliced
250g punnet yellow teardrop
   tomatoes

CREAMY HORSERADISH
⅓ cup French dressing
1 teaspoon horseradish cream
1 tablespoon mayonnaise
1 tablespoon sour light cream
2 tablespoons chopped fresh chives

Trim excess fat from beef. Heat oil in pan, add beef, cook over high heat until well browned all over.

Place beef in baking dish, bake in moderate oven for about 25 minutes or until medium rare; cool.

Add pasta to large pan of boiling water, boil, uncovered, until just tender, drain, rinse under cold water; drain well.

Boil, steam or microwave peas until just tender; drain. Cut beef into cubes, combine beef cubes with pasta, peas, pepper, tomatoes and creamy horseradish in bowl; toss gently.

Creamy Horseradish: Combine all ingredients in jar; shake well.

Serves 6.

■ Salad can be made 3 hours ahead.
■ Storage: Covered, in refrigerator.
■ Freeze: Not suitable.
■ Microwave: Pasta and peas suitable.

GOLDEN PASTA BITES WITH GARLIC MAYONNAISE

2 cups (160g) fusilli pasta
plain flour
2 eggs, lightly beaten
packaged breadcrumbs
oil for deep-frying

GARLIC MAYONNAISE
3 egg yolks
2 teaspoons dry mustard
1 tablespoon white vinegar
2 cloves garlic, crushed
1½ cups olive oil
1 tablespoon finely chopped
    red pepper
1 tablespoon chopped fresh chives
1 tablespoon chopped fresh parsley

Add pasta to large pan of boiling water, boil, uncovered, until just tender, drain, rinse well under cold water; pat dry with absorbent paper. Lightly toss pasta in flour, shake away excess flour. Dip pasta in eggs then breadcrumbs.

Just before serving, deep-fry pasta in hot oil until lightly browned; drain on absorbent paper. Serve hot pasta with garlic mayonnaise.

Garlic Mayonnaise: Blend or process egg yolks, mustard, vinegar and garlic until smooth. With motor operating, add oil gradually in thin stream, blend until thick. Transfer mixture to bowl, stir in pepper and herbs.

Serves 4.

■ Pasta can be prepared a day ahead. Mayonnaise can be made a day ahead.
■ Storage: Covered, in refrigerator.
■ Freeze: Not suitable.
■ Microwave: Not suitable.

ABOVE LEFT: Clockwise from front: Sherried Ham Pots with Sultana Citrus Sauce, Warm Salmon and Asparagus Salad, Beef and Pasta Salad with Creamy Horseradish.

Serving ware from Butler & Co.

SHERRIED HAM POTS WITH SULTANA CITRUS SAUCE

¼ quantity plain pasta dough
200g butter
300g leg ham, chopped
1 onion, chopped
4 green shallots, chopped
2 teaspoons canned drained
    green peppercorns
pinch cayenne pepper
¼ cup sweet sherry
½ cup cream
2½ teaspoons gelatine
1 tablespoon water

SULTANA CITRUS SAUCE
1 cup water
2½ teaspoons cornflour
¼ cup port wine jelly
1 teaspoon grated orange rind
¼ cup orange juice
2 tablespoons sultanas

Lightly oil 6 moulds (½ cup capacity). Roll pasta dough until 1mm thick. Add pasta sheet to large pan of boiling water, boil, uncovered, until just tender; drain, cool. Cut 6 x 11cm rounds from pasta, line prepared moulds with pasta rounds.

Heat butter in pan, add ham, onion, shallots, peppercorns and cayenne, cook, stirring, until onion is soft. Add sherry and cream, bring to boil, simmer, uncovered, for about 5 minutes or until slightly thickened; cool.

Sprinkle gelatine over water in cup, stand in small pan of simmering water, stir until dissolved; cool slightly. Combine ham mixture and gelatine, blend or process mixture until smooth, spoon into moulds; cover, refrigerate several hours or until firm.

Just before serving, turn out moulds, serve with sauce.

Sultana Citrus Sauce: Blend 2 tablespoons of the water with cornflour in bowl. Combine remaining water with remaining ingredients in pan, bring to boil, stir in cornflour mixture, stir until sauce boils and thickens; cover, cool. Refrigerate sauce until cold.

Serves 6.

■ Ham pots and sauce can be made 2 days ahead.
■ Storage: Covered, in refrigerator.
■ Freeze: Not suitable.
■ Microwave: Pasta, gelatine and sauce suitable.

BELOW: Golden Pasta Bites with Garlic Mayonnaise.

FRIED PASTA BOWS WITH PORK AND PLUM SAUCE

1 cup (70g) farfalle pasta
plain flour
2 eggs, lightly beaten
packaged breadcrumbs
oil for deep-frying

PORK AND PLUM SAUCE
2 teaspoons light soy sauce
2 teaspoons hoi sin sauce
1/3 cup plum sauce
1/4 teaspoon sesame oil
2 tablespoons plum jam
1/4 cup water
1/4 teaspoon sambal oelek
1 teaspoon cornflour
2 teaspoons dry sherry
250g piece barbecued
    red pork, sliced

Add pasta to large pan of boiling water, boil, uncovered, until just tender, drain well, pat dry with absorbent paper. Toss pasta in flour, shake away excess flour, dip in eggs then breadcrumbs. Place crumbed pasta in single layer on tray; cover, refrigerate 1 hour.

Just before serving, deep-fry pasta in hot oil until well browned; drain on absorbent paper, serve with sauce.

Pork and Plum Sauce: Combine sauces, oil, jam, water and sambal oelek in pan. Stir in blended cornflour and sherry, stir over heat until sauce boils and thickens, stir in pork, cook until pork is heated through.

    Serves 4.

■ Pasta can be crumbed a day ahead.
  Sauce can be made a day ahead.
■ Storage: Covered, in refrigerator.
■ Freeze: Not suitable.
■ Microwave: Sauce suitable.

PRAWN AND NOODLE SOUP

30g butter
1 red pepper, chopped
1 onion, chopped
1 leek, chopped
2 x 410g cans tomatoes
1½ teaspoons grated fresh ginger
2 small chicken stock cubes,
    crumbled
2 litres (8 cups) water
1 tablespoon chopped fresh parsley
tiny   pinch saffron
2 tablespoons tomato paste
1 carrot
1 stick celery
50g fresh egg noodles
1 teaspoon cracked black
    peppercorns
1½ tablespoons lemon juice
75g oyster mushrooms
300g cooked prawns, shelled

Heat butter in large pan, add pepper, onion and leek, cook, stirring, for about 10 minutes or until leek is soft. Stir in undrained crushed tomatoes, ginger, stock cubes, water, parsley, saffron and paste. Bring to boil, simmer, uncovered, for about 40 minutes or until liquid is reduced by two-thirds. Strain mixture, reserve stock; discard pulp. Cut carrot and celery into strips.

Just before serving, return stock to pan, bring to boil, add carrot, celery, noodles, peppercorns and juice. Simmer, covered, for 5 minutes, add mushrooms and prawns, cook further 2 minutes.

    Serves 4.

■ Recipe can be prepared a day ahead.
■ Storage: Covered, in refrigerator.
■ Freeze: Not suitable.
■ Microwave: Suitable.

LEFT: From left: Fried Pasta Bows with Pork and Plum Sauce, Prawn and Noodle Soup.

LEAFY PASTA SQUARES IN BUTTER WITH PARMESAN

1/2 cup plain flour
2 tablespoons fine semolina
1/4 cup finely grated fresh
    parmesan cheese
1 egg
20 flat-leafed parsley leaves
100g fresh parmesan cheese, extra
90g butter

Sift flour and semolina into bowl, stir in grated cheese. Add egg, stir until combined (or process all ingredients until smooth). Turn dough onto lightly floured surface, knead until smooth. Roll dough through pasta machine, following manufacturer's instructions, until 2mm thick. Lay pasta sheet on bench, press leaves over half the pasta, fold pasta in half crossways over leaves. Roll pasta through machine once, cut pasta into 3cm squares.

Just before serving, add pasta to large pan of boiling water, boil, uncovered, until just tender; drain.

Use vegetable peeler to shave strips from extra parmesan. Melt butter in pan, add pasta, heat through. Serve pasta topped with strips of parmesan.

Serves 4.

■ Squares can be made 6 hours ahead.
■ Storage: Covered, in refrigerator.
■ Freeze: Uncooked pasta suitable.
■ Microwave: Not suitable.

CHICKEN AND FENNEL SHELLS WITH CHILLI CHIVE DRESSING

3 large carrots
1 cup water
1 small chicken stock cube, crumbled
2 chicken breast fillets
12 extra large pasta shells

FENNEL FILLING
30g butter
2 onions, finely chopped
1 cup finely chopped fennel bulb
2/3 cup creamed ricotta cheese
2 tablespoons chopped fresh
    fennel leaves
2 tablespoons chopped black olives

CHILLI CHIVE DRESSING
1/2 cup olive oil
1 tablespoon red wine vinegar
1 teaspoon sweet chilli sauce
1 teaspoon sugar
1 tablespoon orange juice
1 tablespoon chopped fresh chives

Using vegetable peeler, cut carrots into thin ribbons. Add carrots to pan of boiling water, drain immediately, rinse under cold water; drain.

Combine water and stock cube in pan, bring to boil. Add chicken, simmer, covered, about 5 minutes or until chicken is just tender, drain; cool. Cut chicken into thin strips, combine with carrots.

Just before serving, add pasta to large pan of boiling water, boil, uncovered, until just tender; drain. Spoon filling into each shell, serve shells over carrot and chicken; top with dressing.

Fennel Filling: Heat butter in pan, add onions and fennel bulb, cook over low heat, stirring occasionally, for about 10 minutes or until onions are lightly browned and soft. Combine onion mixture with cheese, fennel leaves and olives.

Chilli Chive Dressing: Combine all ingredients in jar; shake well.

Serves 4.

■ Can be prepared a day ahead.
■ Storage: Covered, in refrigerator.
■ Freeze: Not suitable.
■ Microwave: Suitable.

LEFT: From left: Leafy Pasta Squares in Butter with Parmesan, Chicken and Fennel Shells with Chilli Chive Dressing.
ABOVE RIGHT: Roast Duck with Tangy Marmalade Sauce.

Left: China from Villeroy & Boch

ROAST DUCK WITH TANGY MARMALADE SAUCE

½ cup orange juice
2 teaspoons hoi sin sauce
¼ teaspoon five spice powder
2 large (500g) duck breast fillets
6 Chinese dried mushrooms
1 cup boiling water
2 small chicken stock cubes,
    crumbled
1 tablespoon orange marmalade
1 teaspoon cornflour
2 teaspoons Grand Marnier
100g snow peas
250g lasagnette pasta

Combine juice, sauce and spice powder in bowl, add duck; cover, refrigerate several hours or overnight, turning occasionally.

Just before serving, remove duck from marinade; reserve marinade. Place duck on rack over baking dish, bake in hot oven for about 15 minutes or until duck is well browned and tender; remove from oven, slice thinly.

While duck is cooking, place mushrooms in bowl, cover with the boiling water, stand 20 minutes. Drain mushrooms, reserve liquid; discard stems, slice caps thinly. Combine mushrooms, reserved liquid, reserved marinade, stock cubes and marmalade in pan. Bring to

boil, simmer, covered, for 5 minutes. Stir in blended cornflour and liqueur, stir until sauce boils and thickens.

Boil, steam or microwave peas until just tender; drain. Add pasta to large pan of boiling water, boil, uncovered, until just tender; drain. Combine pasta and peas, serve with duck and mushrooms, drizzle with hot sauce.

Serves 6.

■ Can be prepared 2 days ahead.
■ Storage: Covered, in refrigerator.
■ Freeze: Not suitable.
■ Microwave: Pasta and snow peas suitable.

21

CRISP PEPPER PASTA WITH PEPPER BEEF FILLING

⅓ cup finely grated gruyere cheese
¼ cup finely grated tasty cheese
¼ teaspoon canned drained green
    peppercorns, crushed
1 teaspoon water, approximately
1 teaspoon olive oil
1 small onion, chopped
100g minced beef
1½ teaspoons tomato paste
3 teaspoons water, extra
1 small beef stock cube, crumbled
½ teaspoon sugar
1 egg, separated
⅓ quantity pepper pasta dough
plain flour
oil for shallow-frying

PORT SAUCE
½ cup port
1 teaspoon canned drained
    green peppercorns
1 cup cream
2 teaspoons cornflour
2 teaspoons water

Combine cheeses and peppercorns in bowl with enough water to make ingredients cling together. Heat olive oil in pan, add onion, cook, stirring, until soft. Add mince, cook, stirring, until well browned. Stir in combined paste, extra water, stock cube and sugar, cook for 3 minutes; cool. Stir in egg white.

Roll pasta dough until 2mm thick, cut into 7cm rounds. Add rounds to large pan of boiling water, boil, uncovered, until just tender; drain well.

Toss rounds in flour, shake away excess flour. Top each round with ½ level teaspoon of cheese mixture and 1 level teaspoon of meat mixture. Brush edges of rounds with egg yolk, fold in half, press edges together firmly.

Just before serving, shallow-fry in hot oil until lightly browned; drain on absorbent paper. Serve with hot sauce.

Port Sauce: Bring port to boil in pan, simmer, uncovered, until reduced by one-third. Stir in peppercorns, cream and blended cornflour and water, stir until sauce boils and thickens.

Serves 6.

■ Can be prepared 2 days ahead.
■ Storage: Covered, in refrigerator.
■ Freeze: Sauce suitable.
■ Microwave: Sauce suitable.

TASTY LITTLE HAM, CHEESE AND PASTA CUPS

2 cups water
2 small chicken stock cubes,
    crumbled
125g bavette pasta
1 cup (100g) finely grated pecorino
    cheese
100g leg ham, finely chopped
½ cup coarsely grated carrot
1 tablespoon chopped fresh parsley
1 tablespoon chopped fresh chives
2 tablespoons chopped stuffed olives
4 eggs, lightly beaten
1½ cups milk

Lightly grease 6 moulds (¾ cup capacity). Combine water and stock cubes in pan, bring to boil, add pasta, boil, uncovered, until just tender; cool pasta in stock.

Combine cheese, ham, carrot, herbs, olives, eggs and milk in large bowl. Add undrained pasta mixture, stir until just combined. Divide mixture between prepared moulds. Stand moulds in baking dish, pour in enough boiling water to come halfway up sides of moulds. Bake, uncovered, in moderate oven for about 1 hour or until firm; cool to room temperature before serving.

Serves 6.

■ Cups can be made 6 hours ahead.
■ Storage: Covered, at room
    temperature.
■ Freeze: Not suitable.
■ Microwave: Not suitable.

SMOKED CHICKEN AND PASTA TERRINE

1 leek
3 x 8cm x 18cm dried lasagne
    pasta sheets
¼ cup olive oil
1 clove garlic, crushed
3 tablespoons tomato paste
1 teaspoon sugar
80g mushrooms, sliced
2 large tomatoes, peeled, seeded
½ cup (90g) black olives, sliced
1 tablespoon drained chopped capers
½ teaspoon dried marjoram leaves
¼ cup plain flour
¼ cup water
1½ cups (150g) grated
    mozzarella cheese
350g smoked chicken breasts, sliced

BASIL DRESSING.
1½ cups olive oil
⅓ cup lemon juice
1½ tablespoons shredded fresh basil
1 small red pepper, chopped

Lightly grease 11cm x 25cm ovenproof glass loaf dish. Wash leek, drop 6 outer leaves of leek into pan of boiling water, boil for 3 minutes, drain; cool. Thinly slice white section of remaining leek.

Add pasta to large pan of boiling water, boil, uncovered, until just tender; drain, rinse under cold water; drain well.

Heat oil in pan, add sliced leek and garlic, cook, stirring, until leek is soft. Add paste, sugar, mushrooms, tomatoes, olives, capers and marjoram. Cook, covered, for 5 minutes, stirring occasionally. Stir in blended flour and water, stir until mixture boils and thickens; cover, cool.

Line base and sides of prepared dish with boiled leek leaves, allowing ends to overhang sides of dish.

Combine cheese and chicken, divide mixture into 4 portions. Sprinkle 1 portion of cheese mixture over base of dish. Trim pasta to fit dish, place a layer of pasta over cheese mixture. Spread with one-third of tomato mixture, top with another portion of cheese mixture. Repeat layering, ending

with cheese mixture. Fold leek leaves over to cover cheese mixture, cover dish with greased foil. Bake in moderate oven for about 1½ hours or until firm to touch; cool, refrigerate overnight.

Just before serving, turn terrine out, serve sliced with dressing.

Basil Dressing: Combine all ingredients in jar; shake well.

Serves 6.

■ Terrine can be made 2 days ahead. Dressing can be made a day ahead.
■ Storage: Covered, in refrigerator.
■ Freeze: Not suitable.
■ Microwave: Not suitable.

LEFT: From left: Crisp Pepper Pasta with Pepper Beef Filling, Tasty Little Ham, Cheese and Pasta Cups.
BELOW: Smoked Chicken and Pasta Terrine.

Left: Plates from Villa Italiana

POULTRY & RABBIT

In this section, we have used chicken, spatchcocks, quail, duck and rabbit in innovative main meals for the family and for entertaining. There are taste treats of many kinds: plump little ravioli and tortellini with delicious fillings, simple baked or fried dishes, curries, stir-fries, casseroles, salads and more. Most are saucy, and all include pasta as part of the dish or as an accompaniment.

CHICKEN SAVARIN WITH CREAMY CURRY SAUCE

200g lasagne verdi pasta sheets
6 chicken breast fillets, chopped
2 egg whites
2 teaspoons brandy
300ml carton cream
1 tablespoon chopped fresh chives
2 teaspoons canned drained green peppercorns, crushed

CREAMY CURRY SAUCE
20g butter
2 teaspoons curry powder
2 teaspoons plain flour
¾ cup milk
½ small chicken stock cube, crumbled
60g packaged cream cheese

Line 24cm savarin pan with plastic wrap. Add pasta to large pan of boiling water, boil, uncovered, until just tender; drain.

Line prepared pan with pasta sheets, overlapping edges, allowing excess pasta to overhang side of pan.

Process chicken, egg whites and brandy until smooth. Add cream, process until just combined; stir in chives and peppercorns. Spread chicken mixture evenly into pan, fold overhanging pasta over mixture, trim edges.

Cover pan with plastic wrap, then foil. Place pan in baking dish, pour enough boiling water into dish to come halfway up side of pan. Bake in moderate oven for about 1½ hours or until firm to touch.

Stand savarin in pan 5 minutes before turning out. Serve with sauce.

Creamy Curry Sauce: Heat butter in pan, stir in curry powder and flour, stir over heat until bubbling. Remove from heat, gradually stir in milk, stock cube and cheese, stir over heat until mixture boils and thickens. Blend or process sauce until smooth.

Serves 6.

■ Savarin and sauce can be made a day ahead.
■ Storage: Covered, in refrigerator.
■ Freeze: Not suitable
■ Microwave: Sauce suitable.

RED CHICKEN CURRY WITH RICE VERMICELLI

250g rice vermicelli
oil for deep-frying
2 tablespoons oil, extra
1kg chicken thigh fillets, chopped
½ cup coconut cream
1 tablespoon chopped fresh coriander

RED CURRY PASTE
1 small red Spanish onion, chopped
2 cloves garlic, crushed
1 teaspoon chopped fresh coriander root
1½ teaspoons dried chilli flakes
2 teaspoons grated fresh ginger
1 teaspoon grated lime rind
2 tablespoons lime juice
3 teaspoons paprika
1 teaspoon ground cumin

Deep-fry vermicelli in hot oil in batches until puffed; drain on absorbent paper.

Heat extra oil in wok or pan, add curry paste, cook, stirring, for 1 minute. Add chicken in batches, stir-fry until chicken is tender. Stir in coconut cream and coriander, bring to boil, simmer, uncovered, for about 5 minutes or until thickened. Serve curry over vermicelli.

Curry Paste: Blend or process all ingredients until smooth.

Serves 6.

■ Curry can be made a day ahead. Paste can be made a week ahead.
■ Storage: Covered, in refrigerator.
■ Freeze: Not suitable.
■ Microwave: Not suitable.

RIGHT: From left: Chicken Savarin with Creamy Curry Sauce, Red Chicken Curry with Rice Vermicelli.
Plates from Butler & Co

ROAST SPATCHCOCKS
WITH PROSCIUTTO SAUCE

3 x Size 4 spatchcocks
2 tablespoons olive oil
500g lasagnette pasta

PROSCIUTTO SAUCE
2 tablespoons olive oil
30g butter
2 onions, chopped
2 cloves garlic, crushed
2 sticks celery, chopped
1 carrot, chopped
1 red pepper, chopped
100g prosciutto, chopped
2 x 410g cans tomatoes
½ cup dry red wine
1 tablespoon tomato paste
2 tablespoons chopped fresh basil

Cut spatchcocks into quarters, place on rack over baking dish, brush spatchcocks with oil, bake in moderately hot oven for about 20 minutes or until tender.

Add pasta to large pan of boiling water, boil, uncovered, until just tender; drain. Serve spatchcocks with pasta and sauce.
Prosciutto Sauce: Heat oil and butter in pan, add onions, garlic, celery, carrot, pepper and prosciutto, cook, stirring, for about 5 minutes or until vegetables are soft. Stir in undrained crushed tomatoes, wine and paste, bring to boil, simmer, uncovered, for about 10 minutes or until sauce is thickened; stir in basil.

Serves 6.

■ Sauce can be made a day ahead.
■ Storage: Covered, in refrigerator.
■ Freeze: Not suitable.
■ Microwave: Pasta suitable.

LEMONY CHICKEN
AND ANCHOVY RAVIOLI

2 teaspoons olive oil
250g minced chicken
4 anchovy fillets, chopped
2 tablespoons grated fresh parmesan cheese
1 tablespoon cream
¼ teaspoon ground nutmeg
1 teaspoon grated lemon rind
2 tablespoons lemon juice
¼ cup chopped fresh parsley
1 quantity plain pasta dough
60g fresh parmesan cheese, thinly sliced, extra

CREAMY CHEESE SAUCE
30g butter
2 tablespoons plain flour
1 cup water
1 small chicken stock cube, crumbled
300ml carton cream
2 tablespoons grated fresh
**   parmesan cheese**

Heat oil in pan, add chicken, cook, stirring, for 2 minutes. Stir in anchovies, cheese, cream, nutmeg, rind, juice and parsley. Blend or process mixture until smooth.

Divide pasta dough in half, roll each piece until 2mm thick. Place ¼ level teaspoons of filling 3cm apart over 1 sheet of pasta. Lightly brush remaining pasta sheet with water, place over filling; press firmly between filling. Cut into square ravioli shapes. Lightly sprinkle ravioli with a little flour.

Just before serving, add ravioli to large pan of boiling water, boil, uncovered, for about 5 minutes or until just tender; drain. Combine ravioli with hot sauce; serve topped with extra cheese.

Creamy Cheese Sauce: Melt butter in pan, add flour, stir over heat until bubbling. Remove from heat, gradually stir in com-bined water and stock cube, stir over heat until mixture boils and thickens. Simmer, uncovered, until reduced by half. Just before serving, stir in cream and cheese.
   Serves 4.

■ Ravioli and sauce can be prepared a day ahead.
■ Storage: Covered, in refrigerator.
■ Freeze: Uncooked ravioli suitable.
■ Microwave: Not suitable.

CHICKEN JAMBALAYA

4 chicken breast fillets
2 tablespoons olive oil
1 onion, chopped
1 clove garlic, crushed
1 small green pepper, chopped
410g can tomatoes
2 small chicken stock cubes,
**   crumbled**
2 cups water
1 cup risoni pasta
¼ teaspoon chilli powder
½ teaspoon seasoned pepper
¼ teaspoon dried thyme leaves
100g leg ham, chopped
¼ cup black olives, chopped

Cut chicken into 1cm strips. Heat oil in pan, add chicken, cook, stirring, until lightly browned and tender; drain chicken on absorbent paper.

Add onion, garlic and green pepper to pan, cook, stirring, until onion is soft. Stir in undrained crushed tomatoes, stock cubes, water, pasta, chilli, seasoned pepper and thyme. Bring to boil, simmer, covered, for about 10 minutes or until pasta is tender.

Add chicken, ham and olives to pan, simmer, covered, further 10 minutes or until most of the liquid has been absorbed.
   Serves 4.

■ Recipe can be made a day ahead.
■ Storage: Covered, in refrigerator.
■ Freeze: Suitable.
■ Microwave: Suitable.

LEFT: From back: Roast Spatchcocks with Prosciutto Sauce, Lemony Chicken and Anchovy Ravioli.
BELOW: Chicken Jambalaya.

CHICKEN TORTELLINI WITH CREAMY TOMATO SAUCE

2 quantities plain pasta dough
1 egg white, lightly beaten

FILLING
500g chicken thigh fillets
2 egg yolks
2 tablespoons chopped fresh basil
½ teaspoon cracked black peppercorns

CREAMY TOMATO SAUCE
1 tablespoon olive oil
1 small onion, chopped
1 clove garlic, crushed
410g can tomatoes
2 tablespoons dry red wine
1 tablespoon chopped fresh basil
½ teaspoon sugar
¼ teaspoon ground black peppercorns
1 cup cream

Roll pasta dough until 2mm thick, cut into 5½cm squares. Brush edges of squares with egg white, top each square with ½ level teaspoon of filling, fold squares in half diagonally, press edges together firmly. Overlap corners of each tortellini, press firmly.

Just before serving, add tortellini to large pan of boiling water, boil, uncovered, for about 4 minutes or until tender. Serve tortellini with sauce.

Filling: Trim excess fat from chicken, process or mince chicken until finely minced. Combine chicken, egg yolks, basil and pepper in bowl; mix well.

Creamy Tomato Sauce: Heat oil in pan, add onion and garlic, cook, stirring, until onion is soft. Stir in undrained crushed tomatoes, wine, basil, sugar and pepper, bring to boil. Blend or process mixture until smooth, return to pan. Stir in cream, cook until heated through.

Serves 4.

■ Tortellini and sauce can be prepared a day ahead.
■ Storage: Covered, in refrigerator.
■ Freeze: Uncooked tortellini suitable.
■ Microwave: Not suitable.

CHILLI CHICKEN AND PASTA STIR-FRY

500g chicken thigh fillets
plain flour
oil for deep-frying
1 tablespoon olive oil
1 onion, chopped
1 clove garlic, crushed
1 small fresh red chilli, finely chopped
2 stems lemon grass, chopped
1 cup (80g) fusilli pasta
2 tablespoons fish sauce
⅓ cup coconut milk
¼ cup shredded fresh basil

Cut chicken into thin strips, toss chicken in flour, shake away excess flour. Deep-fry chicken in hot oil until lightly browned; drain on absorbent paper.

Heat olive oil in pan or wok, add onion, garlic, chilli and lemon grass, stir-fry until onion is soft.

Add pasta to large pan of boiling water, boil, uncovered, until just tender; drain.

Add pasta, sauce, coconut milk and basil to pan, stir-fry until heated through.

Serves 4.

■ Best made just before serving.
■ Freeze: Not suitable.
■ Microwave: Pasta suitable.

CRUMBED FRIED CHICKEN WITH SPICY PEANUT SAUCE

200g fettucine pasta
1 carrot
½ small leek
1 small red pepper
4 chicken breast fillets
plain flour
2 eggs, lightly beaten
packaged breadcrumbs
¼ cup olive oil

SPICY PEANUT SAUCE
2 tablespoons olive oil
1 onion, finely chopped
1 clove garlic, crushed
2 teaspoons curry powder
½ teaspoon turmeric
1 cup water
1 teaspoon white vinegar
2 teaspoons sugar
¼ cup smooth peanut butter

Add pasta to large pan of boiling water, boil, uncovered, until just tender, drain; keep warm. Cut carrot, leek and pepper into thin strips.

Toss chicken in flour, shake away excess flour. Dip chicken in eggs, then breadcrumbs.

Just before serving, heat oil in pan, add chicken, cook until well browned and cooked through. Serve hot with pasta, uncooked vegetable strips and hot sauce.

Spicy Peanut Sauce: Heat oil in pan, add onion and garlic, cook, stirring, until onion is soft. Stir in curry and turmeric, cook for 1 minute. Stir in water, vinegar, sugar and peanut butter, stir until sauce boils and thickens.

Serves 4.

■ Chicken can be crumbed a day ahead. Sauce can be made a day ahead.
■ Storage: Covered, in refrigerator.
■ Freeze: Not suitable.
■ Microwave: Pasta suitable.

LEFT: Clockwise from left: Chicken Tortellini with Creamy Tomato Sauce, Chilli Chicken and Pasta Stir-Fry, Crumbed Fried Chicken with Spicy Peanut Sauce.

Plates, jug and bowl from Corso de Fiori

BAKED QUAIL WITH NUTTY BACON SEASONING

2 cups dry red wine
1 cup olive oil
2 cloves garlic, crushed
2 tablespoons chopped fresh sage
8 quail
2 cups (250g) farfalline pasta

NUTTY BACON SEASONING
4 bacon rashers, chopped
2 tablespoons chopped fresh chives
½ cup stale breadcrumbs
¼ cup pine nuts, toasted

Combine wine, oil, garlic and sage in bowl, add quail; cover, refrigerate several hours or overnight, turning occasionally.

Remove quail from marinade, reserve 1 cup of marinade. Spoon seasoning into quail cavities, secure legs with string. Place quail on wire rack in baking dish, bake in moderate oven for about 35 minutes or until tender.

Add pasta to large pan of boiling water, boil, uncovered, until just tender; drain. Bring reserved marinade to boil in pan, combine with pasta. Serve quail with pasta.

Nutty Bacon Seasoning: Combine bacon, chives, breadcrumbs and nuts in bowl; mix well.

Serves 4.

- Can be prepared a day ahead.
- Storage: Covered, in refrigerator.
- Freeze: Not suitable.
- Microwave: Pasta suitable.

CREAMY HERBED CHICKEN WITH SPINACH SPAGHETTI

4 chicken breast fillets, sliced
2 teaspoons paprika
1 teaspoon cracked black
    peppercorns
250g packet cream cheese
⅓ cup grated fresh parmesan cheese
1 cup water
1 small chicken stock cube, crumbled
1 tablespoon chopped fresh basil
1 tablespoon chopped fresh parsley
1 tablespoon chopped fresh mint
40g butter
500g spinach spaghetti pasta

Combine chicken, paprika and peppercorns in bowl; stand 20 minutes.

Blend or process cheeses, water, stock cube and herbs until almost smooth. Melt butter in pan, add chicken mixture, cook, stirring, over high heat until well browned. Add cheese mixture, bring to boil, simmer, uncovered, for 5 minutes.

Add pasta to large pan of boiling water, boil, uncovered, until just tender; drain. Serve pasta with creamy chicken.

Serves 6.

- Best made just before serving.
- Freeze: Not suitable.
- Microwave: Pasta suitable.

CREAMY ONION CHICKEN ON LINGUINE

1 tablespoon olive oil
20g butter
1 clove garlic, crushed
6 chicken breast fillets
500g linguine pasta
1 onion, chopped
1 small chicken stock cube, crumbled
½ cup water
300ml carton cream
6 green shallots, chopped
1 cup (100g) grated pecorino cheese

Heat oil, butter and garlic in pan, add chicken, cook on both sides until tender. Remove from pan, slice thinly; keep warm. Reserve oil mixture in pan.

Add pasta to large pan of boiling water, boil, uncovered, until just tender, drain.

Reheat oil mixture in pan, add onion, cook, stirring, until onion is soft. Add stock cube and water, bring to boil, simmer, uncovered, until reduced by half. Add cream, shallots and cheese, stir until cheese has melted. Serve chicken on pasta, top with sauce.

Serves 6.

- Recipe best made close to serving.
- Freeze: Not suitable.
- Microwave: Pasta suitable.

LEFT: From back: Baked Quail with Nutty Bacon Seasoning, Creamy Herbed Chicken with Spinach Spaghetti.
ABOVE: Creamy Onion Chicken on Linguine.

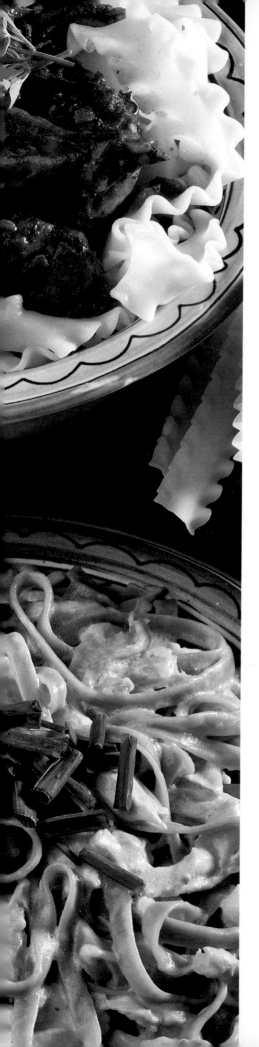

RABBIT IN RED WINE
AND GARLIC SAUCE

1kg rabbit
1 cup dry red wine
1 tablespoon brown sugar
3 bay leaves
4 cloves garlic, sliced
1 tablespoon chopped fresh thyme
2 tablespoons olive oil
1 onion, chopped
200g prosciutto, chopped
410g can tomatoes
2 tablespoons tomato paste
500g lasagnette pasta

Cut rabbit into 8 portions, combine with wine, sugar, bay leaves, garlic and thyme in bowl. Cover, refrigerate 2 hours, stirring occasionally.

Remove rabbit from marinade, drain well; reserve marinade. Heat oil in pan, add rabbit, cook until well browned all over, remove from pan. Add onion and prosciutto to pan, cook, stirring, until onion is soft. Add undrained crushed tomatoes and paste, cook, stirring, for 3 minutes. Stir in reserved marinade, bring to boil, boil 2 minutes. Return rabbit to pan, simmer, covered, for 1 hour, remove cover, simmer further 15 minutes or until sauce is thickened.

Add pasta to large pan of boiling water, boil, uncovered, until just tender; drain. Serve pasta with rabbit and sauce.

Serves 4.

■ Rabbit can be cooked 2 days ahead.
■ Storage: Covered, in refrigerator.
■ Freeze: Not suitable.
■ Microwave: Pasta suitable.

SPATCHCOCKS
IN SAFFRON CREAM

2 x Size 5 spatchcocks
1 tablespoon olive oil
500g spinach tagliatelle pasta
¼ cup chopped fresh chives

SAFFRON CREAM
90g butter
⅔ cup grated fresh parmesan cheese
300ml carton cream
tiny pinch saffron powder

Cut spatchcocks in half through backbones and breastbones, place on rack over baking dish, brush with oil. Bake in moderate oven for about 30 minutes or until tender; cool.

Remove meat from spatchcocks, slice finely. Add pasta to large pan of boiling water, boil, uncovered, until just tender; drain. Return pasta to pan; keep warm.

Combine saffron cream, pasta and spatchcocks, serve sprinkled with chives.

Saffron Cream: Melt butter in separate pan, add cheese, cream and saffron, bring to boil, simmer, uncovered, about 5 minutes or until mixture thickens slightly.

Serves 6.

■ Spatchcocks can be cooked a day ahead. Saffron cream best made just before serving.
■ Storage: Covered, in refrigerator.
■ Freeze: Not suitable.
■ Microwave: Pasta suitable.

CHICKEN SALAD
WITH FRESH THYME DRESSING

2 chicken breast fillets
1 cup (125g) fresh or frozen green peas
1 quantity plain pasta dough

FRESH THYME DRESSING
2 egg yolks
2 tablespoons cider vinegar
1 cup olive oil
3 teaspoons chopped fresh thyme

Poach, steam or microwave chicken until tender, cool; cut into thin strips. Boil, steam or microwave peas until tender, drain; cool.

Roll pasta dough until 2mm thick, cut into 3cm ribbons. Add pasta to large pan of boiling water, boil, uncovered, for about 3 minutes or until just tender; drain. Rinse pasta under cold water; drain. Combine chicken, pasta, peas and dressing in bowl; mix gently.

Fresh Thyme Dressing: Blend or process egg yolks and vinegar until smooth. Add oil gradually in thin stream while motor is operating, blend until thick. Stir in thyme.

Serves 4.

■ Can be prepared 2 hours ahead.
■ Storage: Covered, in refrigerator.
■ Freeze: Not suitable.
■ Microwave: Suitable.

LEFT: Clockwise from left: Chicken Salad with Fresh Thyme Dressing, Rabbit in Red Wine and Garlic Sauce, Spatchcocks in Saffron Cream.

Bowls from Country Floors

WHOLEMEAL PASTA STRIPS WITH RABBIT SAUCE

3 bacon rashers, chopped
1 onion, chopped
2 cloves garlic, crushed
1kg rabbit
8 baby carrots
2 sticks celery, sliced
2 cups water
1 large chicken stock cube, crumbled
2/3 cup dry white wine
1 quantity wholemeal pasta dough
2 teaspoons cornflour
1 tablespoon water, extra
2 tablespoons chopped fresh parsley

Cut bacon into 2cm strips, add to pan, cook, stirring, until well browned. Add onion and garlic, cook, stirring, until onion is soft. Cut rabbit into 8 portions, add to pan, cook, stirring, until rabbit is browned all over. Stir in carrots, celery, water, stock cube and wine, bring to boil, simmer, covered, for about 1½ hours or until rabbit is tender.

Roll pasta dough until 2mm thick, cut into 3cm x 30cm strips. Add strips to large pan of boiling water, boil, uncovered, for about 5 minutes or until just tender; drain.

Remove rabbit meat from bones, return meat to pan. Stir in blended cornflour and extra water, stir until mixture boils and thickens slightly. Serve sauce over pasta, sprinkle with parsley.

Serves 4.

■ Sauce can be made 2 days ahead.
■ Storage: Covered, in refrigerator.
■ Freeze: Sauce suitable.
■ Microwave: Pasta suitable.

SHERRIED RABBIT HOTPOT WITH SPINACH FETTUCINE

1.2kg rabbit cutlets
¼ cup olive oil
2 cloves garlic, crushed
3 bacon rashers chopped
2 x 410g cans tomatoes
¼ cup tomato paste
2 teaspoons sugar
1 small fresh red chilli, chopped
2 bay leaves
½ teaspoon dried oregano leaves
¼ cup sweet sherry
300g broccoli, chopped
125g baby mushrooms
250g spinach fettucine pasta

Remove rabbit meat from bones, chop meat into small pieces. Heat oil in pan, add meat, garlic and bacon, cook, stirring, for 5 minutes. Add undrained crushed

ROAST DUCK WITH TOMATO NOODLE NESTS

2 x No. 18 ducks
30g butter, melted

NOODLE NESTS
250g fresh egg noodles
oil for deep-frying

TOMATO WINE SAUCE
30g butter
1 onion, sliced
2 tomatoes, peeled, seeded
½ cup dry red wine
½ cup water
¼ cup tomato paste
2 teaspoons Worcestershire sauce

Place ducks in baking dish, brush with butter. Bake in moderate oven for about 1½ hours, basting occasionally with pan juices, until ducks are tender.

Cut ducks into quarters, serve hot with noodle nests filled with hot sauce.

Noodle Nests: Arrange quarter of the noodles in thin layer over inside of lightly oiled double strainer. Press top strainer onto noodles. Lower strainer into hot oil, holding handles firmly together, deep-fry until noodles are well browned; drain.

Carefully remove basket from strainer. Repeat with remaining noodles.

Tomato Wine Sauce: Melt butter in pan, add onion, cook, stirring, until soft. Add roughly chopped tomatoes, wine, water, paste and sauce. Bring to boil, simmer, uncovered, for about 20 minutes or until slightly thickened.

Serves 4.

■ Noodle nests and sauce can be made a day ahead.
■ Storage: Separately, covered, in refrigerator.
■ Freeze: Sauce suitable.
■ Microwave: Sauce suitable.

tomatoes, paste, sugar, chilli, bay leaves, oregano and sherry. Bring to boil, simmer, covered, for about 1¼ hours or until rabbit is tender. Add broccoli and mushrooms, cook 5 minutes or until broccoli is just tender. Discard bay leaves.

Add pasta to large pan of boiling water, boil, uncovered, until just tender; drain. Serve rabbit mixture with pasta.

Serves 4.

■ Hotpot can be made 2 days ahead.
■ Storage: Covered, in refrigerator.
■ Freeze: Not suitable.
■ Microwave: Pasta suitable.

ABOVE: From left: Wholemeal Pasta Strips with Rabbit Sauce, Sherried Rabbit Hotpot with Spinach Fettucine.
RIGHT: Roast Duck with Tomato Noodle Nests.
Right: China from Villeroy & Boch

HERBED CHICKEN AND PASTA SALAD

1¼ cups (120g) vegeroni
   pasta spirals
2 cups water
2 small chicken stock cubes,
   crumbled
4 chicken breast fillets
½ cup canned drained
   pimientos, sliced
½ cup black olives

DRESSING
1 clove garlic, crushed
¼ cup red wine vinegar
½ cup olive oil
¼ teaspoon cracked black
   peppercorns
2 tablespoons shredded fresh basil

Add pasta to large pan of boiling water, boil; uncovered, until just tender; drain. Rinse pasta under cold water; drain.

Combine water and stock cubes in pan, bring to boil, add chicken, simmer, covered, for about 10 minutes or until cooked through; drain, cool. Cut chicken into 1cm strips.

Combine chicken, pasta, pimientos and olives in bowl, add dressing, toss to combine. Cover salad, refrigerate several hours before serving.
Dressing: Combine all ingredients in jar; shake well.

Serves 4.

■ Salad can be made a day ahead.
■ Storage: Covered, in refrigerator.
■ Freeze: Not suitable.
■ Microwave: Pasta suitable.

CREAMY CHICKEN, PASTA AND ASPARAGUS CASSEROLE

250g fettucine pasta
2 tablespoons olive oil
1 onion, chopped
1 cup (150g) chopped
   cooked chicken
1 red pepper, chopped
2 sticks celery, chopped
1 small chicken stock cube, crumbled
1 cup water
300g carton sour cream
440g can asparagus cuts, drained
½ teaspoon dried oregano leaves
1 cup (125g) grated tasty cheese

Add pasta to large pan of boiling water, boil, uncovered, until just tender; drain. Rinse pasta under cold water; drain well.

Heat oil in large pan, add onion, cook, stirring, until soft. Add chicken, pepper, celery, stock cube and water, bring to boil, simmer 5 minutes. Add cream, asparagus and oregano, cook until heated through.

Spoon half the chicken mixture over base of greased ovenproof dish (7 cup capacity), top with pasta, then remaining chicken mixture. Sprinkle with cheese, bake in a moderate oven for about 30 minutes or until cheese is lightly browned.

Serves 4.

■ Recipe can be made a day ahead.
■ Storage: Covered, in refrigerator.
■ Freeze: Not suitable.
■ Microwave: Pasta suitable.

LEFT: From left: Creamy Chicken, Pasta and Asparagus Casserole, Herbed Chicken and Pasta Salad.

DUCK AND PASTA SOUFFLES

375g tagliatelle pasta
2 duck breast fillets, thinly sliced
2 tablespoons plum sauce
1 tablespoon hoi sin sauce
2 tablespoons olive oil
2 small carrots, coarsely grated
125g baby mushrooms, sliced
2 bunches (24 spears) fresh
    asparagus, sliced
1 teaspoon sesame oil
1 tablespoon light soy sauce
3 eggs, separated
¼ teaspoon five spice powder

Grease 8 ovenproof dishes (1¼ cup capacity). Add pasta to large pan of boiling water, boil, uncovered, until just tender; drain. Combine duck, plum and hoi sin sauces in bowl; cover, refrigerate 2 hours.

Heat half the oil in pan, add duck mixture, cook, stirring, until lightly browned. Remove from pan, drain on absorbent paper. Add remaining oil to pan, add carrots, mushrooms and asparagus, cook, stirring, for 2 minutes. Stir in half the pasta, duck mixture, sesame oil and soy sauce, stir until heated through. Divide mixture between prepared dishes.

Combine remaining pasta with egg yolks and spice in bowl. Beat egg whites in small bowl until soft peaks form, fold into pasta mixture. Spoon into dishes, place on oven tray, bake in moderately hot oven for about 15 minutes or until puffed.

Serves 8.

■ Best made just before serving.
■ Freeze: Not suitable.
■ Microwave: Pasta suitable.

ONION AND RABBIT RAVIOLI WITH FRESH PARMESAN

80g butter
3 large (500g) onions, thinly sliced
1 large carrot, grated
2 tablespoons balsamic vinegar
2 teaspoons brown sugar
700g rabbit
1 tablespoon olive oil
½ cup grated fresh parmesan cheese
1 egg yolk
56 x 8cm square egg pastry sheets
1 egg, lightly beaten
plain flour
⅔ cup grated fresh parmesan
    cheese, extra

Melt butter in pan, add onions and carrot, cook, stirring, until onions are soft. Add vinegar and sugar, cook slowly, uncovered, for about 40 minutes, stirring occasionally, until onions are golden brown. Remove onions from pan; cool.

Remove meat from rabbit; chop meat. Heat oil in pan, add rabbit, cook, stirring, until well browned and tender; cool. Blend or process cheese, egg yolk, onion mixture and rabbit until finely chopped; cover, refrigerate until cold.

Top each pastry sheet with 2 level teaspoons of rabbit mixture. Brush edges of sheets with egg, fold sheets in half, press edges together to seal. Lightly sprinkle ravioli with flour.

Just before serving, add ravioli to large pan of boiling water, boil, uncovered, for about 5 minutes or until just tender; drain. Serve with extra cheese.

Serves 8.

■ Ravioli can be made a day ahead.
■ Storage: Covered, in refrigerator.
■ Freeze: Uncooked ravioli suitable.
■ Microwave: Not suitable.

SPICY CHICKEN STIR-FRY WITH EGG NOODLES

250g dried egg noodles
2 tablespoons oil
500g chicken thigh fillets
2 cloves garlic, crushed
½ teaspoon five spice powder
½ teaspoon ground cumin
½ teaspoon curry powder
1 small fresh red chilli, chopped
1 red pepper, chopped
3 teaspoons sesame oil
2 tablespoons light soy sauce

Add noodles to pan of boiling water, boil, uncovered, until just tender; drain. Add half the oil to noodles, toss gently.

Cut chicken into thin strips. Heat remaining oil in wok or pan, add garlic, spices, chilli and chicken, stir-fry for about 5 minutes or until chicken is almost tender. Stir in pepper, stir-fry 1 minute, stir in noodles, sesame oil and sauce, stir-fry until heated through.

Serves 4.

■ Recipe best made close to serving.
■ Freeze: Not suitable.
■ Microwave: Noodles suitable.

CHICKEN CANNELLONI WITH PRAWN SAUCE

40g butter
¼ cup plain flour
1 cup water
1 small chicken stock cube, crumbled
3 teaspoons seeded mustard
¾ cup frozen peas
2 cups (300g) finely chopped cooked chicken
12 cannelloni pasta
plain flour, extra
1 egg, lightly beaten
packaged breadcrumbs
oil for deep-frying

PRAWN SAUCE
40g butter
2 tablespoons plain flour
2 teaspoons tomato paste
¼ cup dry red wine
1½ cups water
1 small chicken stock cube, crumbled
1 green shallot, finely chopped
12 uncooked king prawns, shelled
1 tablespoon chopped fresh thyme

Melt butter in pan, add flour, stir over heat until lightly browned. Remove from heat, gradually stir in combined water, stock cube and mustard, bring to boil. Stir in peas, simmer, uncovered, for 2 minutes. Stir in chicken; cool.

Add pasta to large pan of boiling water, boil, uncovered, until just tender; drain.

Spoon chicken mixture into piping bag fitted with 2cm plain tube, pipe mixture into pasta. Roll pasta lightly in extra flour, dip in egg, then breadcrumbs. Place on tray; cover, refrigerate for 20 minutes.

Just before serving, deep-fry pasta in batches in hot oil until well browned; drain on absorbent paper. Serve with hot sauce.

Prawn Sauce: Melt butter in pan, add flour, stir over heat until bubbling. Remove from heat, gradually stir in paste, wine, water and stock cube. Stir over heat until mixture boils and thickens, simmer, uncovered, for 5 minutes. Stir in shallot and prawns, simmer further 5 minutes or until prawns are tender; stir in thyme.

Serves 6.

■ Recipe can be prepared a day ahead.
■ Storage: Covered, in refrigerator.
■ Freeze: Not suitable.
■ Microwave: Pasta suitable.

ABOVE LEFT: Clockwise from back: Spicy Chicken Stir-Fry with Egg Noodles, Onion and Rabbit Ravioli with Fresh Parmesan, Duck and Pasta Souffles.
RIGHT: Chicken Cannelloni with Prawn Sauce.

Right: Plate from Villa Italiana

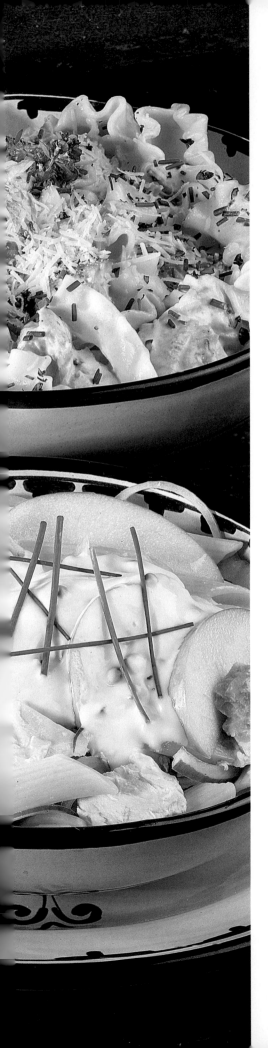

CHICKEN WITH HERBED LEMON SAUCE

350g lasagnette pasta
60g butter
1 teaspoon grated lemon rind
¼ cup lemon juice
300ml carton cream
2 tablespoons chopped fresh chives
1 tablespoon chopped fresh thyme
3 cups (450g) chopped
    cooked chicken
½ cup grated fresh parmesan cheese

Add pasta to large pan of boiling water, boil, uncovered, until just tender; drain.

Heat butter, rind and juice in pan until butter is melted. Add cream, half the herbs, chicken and pasta, stir until heated through. Serve sprinkled with remaining herbs and cheese.

Serves 4.

■ Recipe best made just before serving.
■ Freeze: Not suitable.
■ Microwave: Pasta suitable.

PEPPERED CHICKEN AND PASTA SALAD

100g penne pasta
1 cup (150g) chopped
    cooked chicken
1 red Spanish onion, thinly sliced
1 apple, chopped
2 sticks celery, chopped

DRESSING
1 tablespoon drained canned green
    peppercorns, crushed
⅓ cup cream
¼ cup mayonnaise
½ teaspoon grated lemon rind
1 tablespoon lemon juice
¼ teaspoon sugar

Add pasta to large pan of boiling water, boil, uncovered, until just tender; drain. Rinse pasta under cold water; drain.

Combine pasta, chicken, onion, apple and celery in bowl. Add dressing to pasta mixture, toss well.
Dressing: Combine all ingredients in bowl; mix well.

Serves 4.

■ Salad can be made a day ahead.
■ Storage: Covered, in refrigerator.
■ Freeze: Not suitable.
■ Microwave: Pasta suitable

CHICKEN AND NOODLE PATTIES

¼ cup Chinese dried mushrooms
¼ cup oil
1 large onion, finely chopped
1 clove garlic, crushed
200g fresh egg noodles
4 eggs, lightly beaten
2 teaspoons rice vinegar
1 cup (200g) finely chopped
    cooked chicken
3 green shallots, chopped
2 tablespoons chopped fresh parsley
2 tablespoons cornflour
1 teaspoon sesame oil

ORANGE SAUCE
¼ cup hoi sin sauce
2 tablespoons oyster sauce
2 teaspoons grated orange rind
¼ cup orange juice
2 teaspoons sugar
2 tablespoons water
¼ teaspoon cornflour
1 tablespoon water, extra

Place mushrooms in bowl, cover with boiling water, stand 20 minutes. Drain mushrooms, discard liquid. Discard stems, slice caps thinly.

Heat 1 tablespoon of the oil in pan, add onion and garlic, cook, stirring, until onion is soft; cool. Combine onion mixture, mushrooms, noodles, eggs, vinegar, chicken, shallots, parsley, cornflour and sesame oil in bowl.

Shape ⅓ cup of mixture into a patty, repeat with remaining mixture. Heat remaining oil in pan, add patties, cook until lightly browned on both sides. Serve hot patties with warm sauce.
Orange Sauce: Combine sauces, rind, juice, sugar and water in pan, bring to boil. Stir in blended cornflour and extra water, stir until sauce boils and thickens.

Serves 4.

■ Patties and sauce can be made
    a day ahead.
■ Storage: Covered, in refrigerator.
■ Freeze: Not suitable.
■ Microwave: Sauce suitable.

LEFT: Clockwise from left: Chicken and Noodle Patties, Chicken with Herbed Lemon Sauce, Peppered Chicken and Pasta Salad.

Plates and bowls from Corso de Fiori

SEAFOOD

Fresh seafood is wonderful to cook with because it is usually quick and always popular. Lobster, prawns, mussels, smoked salmon and all your favourites are here in dishes ranging from light and pretty to quite hearty eating (depending on the size of the helping, of course!). Even if you think you "can't cook" you'll find something here that is well within your skills. Again, lovely sauces are important and, in every dish, pasta is seafood's perfect partner, ready to star or be an accompaniment.

GARLIC CREAM MUSSELS WITH RIGATONI

375g rigatoni pasta
1kg mussels
40g butter
1 onion, chopped
3 cloves garlic, crushed
2 red peppers, chopped
½ cup sour cream
¼ cup dry white wine
4 green shallots, finely chopped
2 tablespoons chopped fresh parsley

Add pasta to large pan of boiling water, boil, uncovered, until just tender; drain.

Scrub mussels, remove beards. Melt butter in large pan, add onion, cook, stirring, until soft. Add garlic and peppers, cook, stirring, for 2 minutes. Stir in sour cream and wine, bring to boil. Add mussels, bring to boil, simmer, covered, for about 3 minutes or until shells have opened. Add shallots, parsley and pasta to pan, stir until just heated through.

Serves 6.

■ Recipe best made close to serving.
■ Freeze: Not suitable.
■ Microwave: Suitable.

SALMON CANNELLONI WITH PIMIENTO MINT SAUCE

1½ x 415g cans salmon, drained
180g feta cheese, crumbled
2 sticks celery, chopped
6 green shallots, chopped
⅓ cup mayonnaise
1½ tablespoons lemon juice
12 cannelloni pasta
¼ cup grated fresh parmesan cheese

PIMIENTO MINT SAUCE
410g can tomatoes
185g can pimientos, drained, chopped
1 cup fresh mint leaves
1 tablespoon brown sugar

Remove skin and bones from salmon. Combine salmon, feta cheese, celery, shallots, mayonnaise and juice in bowl; mix well.

Add pasta to large pan of boiling water, boil, uncovered, until just tender; drain.

Spoon salmon mixture into cannelloni, place in greased ovenproof dish in single layer, cover, bake in moderate oven for about 15 minutes or until heated through. Serve cannelloni with hot sauce, sprinkle with parmesan cheese.

Pimiento Mint Sauce: Combine undrained crushed tomatoes, pimientos, mint and sugar in pan. Bring to boil, simmer, uncovered, for about 5 minutes or until mixture is reduced and thickened. Blend or process sauce until smooth.

Serves 4.

■ Recipe can be made a day ahead.
■ Storage: Covered, in refrigerator.
■ Freeze: Not suitable.
■ Microwave: Suitable.

FRESH TUNA CHUNKS IN HOT CHILLI DRESSING

500g piece fresh tuna
2 bay leaves
½ cup olive oil
2 tablespoons lemon juice
1 clove garlic, finely chopped
1 teaspoon cracked black peppercorns
1 tablespoon chopped fresh flat-leafed parsley
20g butter
1 onion, thinly sliced
1 small fresh red chilli, shredded
500g bavette pasta

Cut tuna into 2cm pieces, place into ovenproof dish with bay leaves, oil, juice, garlic, peppercorns and parsley; do not stir. Cover dish, bake in moderate oven for about 20 minutes or until tuna is tender; discard bay leaves.

Melt butter in pan, add onion, cook, stirring, until soft. Stir in chilli and tuna mixture, stir until heated through.

Add pasta to large pan of boiling water, boil, uncovered, until just tender; drain. Serve pasta with tuna mixture.

Serves 4.

■ Best made just before serving.
■ Freeze: Not suitable.
■ Microwave: Suitable.

RIGHT: Clockwise from left: Fresh Tuna Chunks in Hot Chilli Dressing, Salmon Cannelloni with Pimiento Mint Sauce, Garlic Cream Mussels with Rigatoni.

Plates from Villa Italiana

HONEYED SCALLOPS WITH TROPICAL FRUIT SALSA

500g scallops
⅓ cup honey
2 teaspoons chilli sauce
½ cup dry white wine
1 teaspoon grated fresh ginger
250g farfalle pasta
3 teaspoons cornflour
1 tablespoon water

TROPICAL FRUIT SALSA
1½ cups (280g) chopped fresh pineapple
1 cup (220g) chopped fresh mango
1 tablespoon chopped fresh mint

Thread scallops onto small skewers, place in shallow glass dish. Pour combined honey, sauce, wine and ginger over kebabs; cover, refrigerate several hours. Drain kebabs, reserve marinade.
Just before serving, grill or barbecue kebabs until scallops are just tender.

Add pasta to large pan of boiling water, boil, uncovered, until just tender; drain, keep warm.

Combine blended cornflour and water with reserved marinade in pan, stir over heat until mixture boils and thickens.

Serve kebabs on pasta with thickened marinade, serve with tropical fruit salsa.
Tropical Fruit Salsa: Combine all ingredients in bowl; mix gently.
Serves 4.

■ Recipe can be prepared a day ahead.
■ Storage: Covered, in refrigerator.
■ Freeze: Not suitable.
■ Microwave: Pasta suitable.

LEMONY SEAFOOD IN SAFFRON GARLIC SAUCE

1kg mussels
500g uncooked king prawns
½ cup dry white wine
½ cup water
1 lemon
tiny pinch saffron powder
250g fettucine pasta
20g butter
1 tablespoon olive oil
2 cloves garlic, crushed
2 green shallots, chopped
½ cup cream
2 egg yolks
1 tablespoon lemon juice
1 tablespoon chopped fresh oregano

Scrub mussels, remove beards. Shell and devein prawns, leaving tails intact. Combine mussels, wine and water in pan, cover, bring to boil, simmer 1 minute. Strain mussels, reserve liquid.

Thinly peel rind from lemon. Combine rind in pan with reserved liquid and saffron, simmer, uncovered, until liquid is reduced by half. Strain, reserve liquid.

Add pasta to large pan of boiling water, boil, uncovered, until just tender; drain.

Heat butter and oil in pan, add garlic

and shallots, cook, stirring, for 1 minute. Stir in reserved liquid and combined cream and egg yolks, stir, without boiling, until slightly thickened. Stir in seafood, juice and oregano, simmer, covered, for about 2 minutes or until prawns are tender. Serve sauce over pasta.
Serves 4.

■ Sauce can be made a day ahead.
■ Storage: Covered, in refrigerator.
■ Freeze: Not suitable.
■ Microwave: Pasta suitable.

TOMATO, ANCHOVY AND ARTICHOKE SALAD

500g spiral pasta
4 large (1kg) tomatoes, peeled, seeded, chopped
1 cup (185g) black olives, halved
275g jar artichoke hearts, drained, halved
56g can anchovy fillets, drained, chopped

DRESSING
¼ cup olive oil
¼ cup lemon juice
¼ cup chopped fresh basil
2 tablespoons chopped fresh parsley

Add pasta to large pan of boiling water, boil, uncovered, until just tender; drain.

Combine tomatoes, olives, artichokes, anchovies and pasta in bowl, add dressing; toss well.
Dressing: Combine all ingredients in jar; shake well.
Serves 4.

■ Salad can be made a day ahead.
■ Storage: Covered, in refrigerator.
■ Freeze: Not suitable.
■ Microwave: Pasta suitable.

LEFT: From left: Lemony Seafood in Saffron Garlic Sauce, Tomato, Anchovy and Artichoke Salad.
BELOW: Honeyed Scallops with Tropical Fruit Salsa.

Left: Bowls from Powder Blue. Below: Plate from Villa Italiana

SMOKED SALMON TORTELLINI WITH HOT CABBAGE SALAD

1 quantity plain pasta dough
1 egg, lightly beaten

FILLING
1 tablespoon olive oil
1 small onion, chopped
180g smoked salmon pieces, chopped
1½ tablespoons chopped fresh parsley

HOT CABBAGE SALAD
¼ cup olive oil
2 cloves garlic, crushed
1 red pepper, sliced
¼ medium cabbage, shredded
½ teaspoon ground black peppercorns

Roll dough until 2mm thick, cut into 7½cm rounds. Brush rounds with egg, top each round with 1 level teaspoon of filling, fold rounds in half, press edges together to seal. Pinch points together.

Just before serving, add tortellini to large pan of boiling water, boil, uncovered, for about 8 minutes or until just tender; drain. Serve tortellini over cabbage salad.

Filling: Heat oil in pan, add onion, cook, stirring, until soft; cool. Combine onion, salmon and parsley in bowl.

Hot Cabbage Salad: Heat oil in pan, add garlic and pepper, cook, stirring, until pepper is soft. Add cabbage and peppercorns, cook, stirring, until cabbage is soft.

Serves 4.

■ Tortellini can be made a day ahead.
■ Storage: Covered, in refrigerator.
■ Freeze: Cooked tortellini suitable.
■ Microwave: Not suitable.

GINGERED PRAWN AND PEA NOODLES

750g uncooked medium prawns
2 stems fresh lemon grass, finely chopped
1 teaspoon ground coriander
2 teaspoons ground ginger
200g sugar snap peas
500g fresh egg noodles
2 tablespoons oil

BUTTER SAUCE
1 teaspoon cornflour
2½ tablespoons water
⅓ cup sake
2 tablespoons lemon juice
1 teaspoon grated fresh ginger
90g butter

Shell and devein prawns, leaving tails intact. Combine prawns, lemon grass, coriander and ginger in bowl; cover, refrigerate 1 hour.

Boil, steam or microwave peas until tender; drain. Cover noodles with boiling water, stand 5 minutes; drain.

Heat oil in wok or pan, add prawn mixture, stir-fry until prawns are cooked through. Add peas, noodles and butter sauce, stir until heated through.

Butter Sauce: Combine blended cornflour and water with sake, juice and ginger in pan, stir over heat until mixture boils and thickens. Remove from heat, add butter, stir until melted.

Serves 4.

■ Best made just before serving.
■ Freeze: Not suitable.
■ Microwave: Sauce suitable.

LEFT: From left: Gingered Prawn and Pea Noodles, Smoked Salmon Tortellini with Hot Cabbage Salad.

QUICK SEAFOOD SHELLS

24 extra large pasta shells
1 tablespoon olive oil
1 onion, finely chopped
1 large (about 180g) carrot, coarsely
    grated
1 large (about 200g) zucchini,
    coarsely grated
100g baby mushrooms, finely
    chopped
2 tomatoes, finely chopped
¼ cup dry white wine
425g can tuna, drained, mashed
56g can anchovies, drained, chopped
1 cup water
1 small chicken stock cube, crumbled
40g packaged cream cheese,
    chopped
1 tablespoon chopped fresh basil

Add pasta to large pan of boiling water,
boil, uncovered, until just tender; drain.

Heat oil in pan, add onion, cook, stirring,
until soft. Add carrot, zucchini and mushrooms, cook, stirring, until vegetables are
soft. Stir in tomatoes and wine, bring to
boil, simmer, uncovered, about 5 minutes
or until mixture is slightly thickened.

Combine half the vegetable mixture
with tuna and anchovies in bowl, spoon
into pasta shells, place shells in greased
ovenproof dish.

Just before serving, bake shells,
covered, in moderate oven for about 10
minutes or until heated through.

Blend or process remaining vegetable
mixture, water, stock cube and cream
cheese until smooth. Pour mixture into
pan, stir over heat until heated through;
stir in basil. Serve sauce with shells.
    Serves 4.

■ Recipe can be prepared a day ahead.
■ Storage: Covered, in refrigerator.
■ Freeze: Not suitable.
■ Microwave: Suitable.

PASTA MARINARA

30g butter
1 onion, chopped
1 clove garlic, crushed
410g can tomatoes
2 tablespoons tomato paste
1 cup water
1 small chicken stock cube, crumbled
375g paglia e fieno pasta
500g marinara mix
2 tablespoons chopped fresh parsley
¼ cup grated fresh parmesan cheese

Melt butter in pan, add onion and garlic,
cook, stirring, until onion is soft. Add
undrained crushed tomatoes, paste,
water and stock cube. Bring to boil, simmer, uncovered, for about 10 minutes or
until sauce is thickened.

Add pasta to large pan of boiling water,

boil, uncovered, until just tender; drain.

Add marinara mix to sauce, simmer,
uncovered, until seafood is tender.
Remove from heat, stir in parsley and
cheese. Serve sauce over pasta.
    Serves 4.

■ Recipe best made close to serving.
■ Freeze: Not suitable.
■ Microwave: Suitable.

CRAB RAVIOLI WITH TOMATO
AND RED PEPPER SAUCE

1 tablespoon olive oil
6 green shallots, chopped
200g white fish fillets
170g can crab meat, drained, flaked
1½ tablespoons lemon juice
1 tablespoon chopped fresh oregano
¼ cup packaged breadcrumbs
2 egg yolks
60 x 8cm wonton wrappers
1 egg, lightly beaten
½ cup grated fresh parmesan cheese

TOMATO AND RED PEPPER SAUCE
1 red pepper
1 tablespoon olive oil
1 clove garlic, crushed
2 x 410g cans tomatoes
¼ teaspoon sugar
½ teaspoon grated orange rind

Heat oil in pan, add shallots, cook, stirring,
until just soft. Add fish, cook, covered,

SMOKED TROUT AND HONEYDEW SALAD

1½ bunches (18 spears) fresh asparagus
200g sliced smoked trout
1 cup (125g) farfalline pasta
½ honeydew melon, sliced
1 butter lettuce, sliced

STRAWBERRY VINAIGRETTE
½ x 250g punnet strawberries
½ cup olive oil
¼ cup white vinegar
½ teaspoon sugar
¼ teaspoon ground black peppercorns

Boil, steam or microwave asparagus until just tender; drain. Place asparagus in bowl of ice water until cold; drain. Roll trout slices around asparagus.

Add pasta to large pan of boiling water, boil, uncovered, until just tender, drain; rinse under cold water, drain.

Just before serving, place melon, lettuce and pasta on plates, top with trout rolls and vinaigrette.

Strawberry Vinaigrette: Blend or process strawberries until smooth, strain. Combine strawberries with remaining ingredients in jar; shake well.

Serves 4 to 6.

■ Can be prepared 3 hours ahead.
■ Storage: Covered, in refrigerator.
■ Freeze: Not suitable.
■ Microwave: Suitable.

LEFT: Clockwise from left: Quick Seafood Shells, Pasta Marinara, Crab Ravioli with Tomato and Red Pepper Sauce.
BELOW: Smoked Trout and Honeydew Salad.

turning once, until tender. Mash fish in bowl; cool. Add crab, juice, oregano, breadcrumbs and egg yolks to fish, mix well; cover, refrigerate 1 hour.

Top half the wonton wrappers with 2 level teaspoons of crab mixture, brush edges of wrappers with egg, top with remaining wrappers, press edges together to seal.

Just before serving, add ravioli to large pan of boiling water, boil, uncovered, for about 6 minutes or until just tender; drain. Serve ravioli with warm sauce, sprinkled with parmesan cheese.

Tomato and Red Pepper Sauce: Cut pepper into quarters, remove seeds and membrane. Grill pepper, skin side up, until skin blackens and blisters. Peel skin, chop pepper.

Heat oil in pan, add pepper and garlic, cook, stirring, until pepper is soft. Stir in undrained crushed tomatoes and sugar, bring to boil, simmer, uncovered, for about 5 minutes or until thickened. Blend or process mixture until smooth, stir in rind.

Serves 6.

■ Ravioli and sauce can be made a day ahead.
■ Storage: Covered, in refrigerator.
■ Freeze: Uncooked ravioli suitable.
■ Microwave: Not suitable.

SPICY FISH WITH OLIVES AND SUN-DRIED TOMATOES

1/4 cup olive oil
1 onion, thinly sliced
2 cloves garlic, sliced
1 tablespoon chopped drained
  anchovy fillets
1 tablespoon chopped
  drained capers
2 teaspoons sambal oelek
1/4 cup chopped drained sun-dried
  tomatoes
500g white fish fillets, chopped
1/2 cup black olives
375g tomato tagliatelle pasta

Heat oil in pan, add onion and garlic, cook, stirring, until onion is soft. Stir in anchovies, capers, sambal oelek and tomatoes. Add fish to pan, cook over low heat until tender; add olives.

Add pasta to large pan of boiling water, boil, uncovered, until just tender; drain. Serve pasta with fish mixture.

Serves 4.

■ Recipe best made close to serving.
■ Freeze: Not suitable.
■ Microwave: Suitable.

SMOKED SALMON POUCHES WITH PIMIENTO CREAM

100g smoked salmon pieces,
  finely chopped
80g packaged cream cheese,
  softened
1 tablespoon finely chopped canned
  drained pimientos
1 tablespoon lemon juice
1 tablespoon chopped fresh chives
250g packet gow gees pastry

PIMIENTO CREAM
2 tablespoons chopped canned
  drained pimientos
1 teaspoon lemon juice
2 teaspoons chopped fresh dill
1/2 cup cream

Combine salmon, cheese, pimientos, juice and chives in bowl. Top each pastry sheet with 1 level teaspoon of salmon mixture. Brush edges of pastry lightly with water, gather edges together around salmon mixture to form pouches.

Just before serving, add pouches to large pan of boiling water, boil, uncovered, for about 3 minutes or until just tender; drain. Serve pouches with pimiento cream and extra dill, if desired.

Pimiento Cream: Blend or process all ingredients until almost smooth. Transfer mixture to pan, stir over low heat until heated through.

Serves 4.

■ Can be prepared a day ahead.
■ Storage: Covered, in refrigerator.
■ Freeze: Uncooked pouches suitable.
■ Microwave: Pimiento cream suitable.

TOMATO AND PRAWN PASTA BAKES

500g packet vegeroni spiral pasta
2 tablespoons olive oil
60g butter
2 leeks, sliced
4 cloves garlic, crushed
1 teaspoon chilli powder
2 tablespoons chopped
  fresh oregano
2 x 410g cans tomatoes
1/4 cup dry sherry
1kg uncooked prawns,
  shelled, chopped
200g feta cheese, crumbled

Add pasta to large pan of boiling water, boil, uncovered, until just tender; drain.

Heat oil and butter in pan, add leeks, garlic and chilli, cook, stirring, until leeks are soft. Stir in oregano, undrained crushed tomatoes, sherry and prawns, bring to boil, simmer 1 minute. Spoon pasta into 6 greased ovenproof dishes (2 cup capacity), top with prawn mixture, sprinkle with cheese.

Just before serving, bake in moderately hot oven for about 10 minutes or until cheese is browned and pasta heated through.

Serves 6.

■ Can be prepared a day ahead.
■ Storage: Covered, in refrigerator.
■ Freeze: Not suitable.
■ Microwave: Pasta suitable.

RIGHT: Clockwise from back: Smoked Salmon Pouches with Pimiento Cream, Spicy Fish with Olives and Sun-Dried Tomatoes, Tomato and Prawn Pasta Bakes.

Fabric from Les Olivades

FIVE SEAFOODS WITH FENNEL CREAM SAUCE

4 large (about 180g) cooked king
    prawns
30g butter
1 onion, chopped
1 clove garlic, crushed
2 tablespoons plain flour
2 cups milk
300ml carton cream
1 teaspoon fennel seeds, crushed
200g white fish fillets, chopped
200g Atlantic salmon fillet, chopped
150g scallops
150g mussel meat
400g spinach fettucine pasta
3 green shallots, chopped

Shell and devein prawns, leaving heads
and tails intact. Melt butter in pan, add
onion and garlic, cook, stirring, until onion
is soft. Stir in flour, cook until bubbling.
Remove from heat, gradually stir in milk,
cream and fennel. Stir over heat until
sauce boils and thickens slightly. Stir in
seafood, simmer, uncovered, for about 5
minutes or until seafood is tender.

Add pasta to large pan of boiling water,
boil, uncovered, until just tender; drain.
Serve fennel cream sauce over pasta,
sprinkle with shallots.

Serves 4.

■ Recipe best made just before serving.
■ Freeze: Not suitable.
■ Microwave: Suitable.

STIR-FRIED SEAFOOD SALAD

2 tablespoons honey
1 tablespoon light soy sauce
1 tablespoon oyster sauce
1 tablespoon dry sherry
1 teaspoon sesame oil
2 teaspoons grated fresh ginger
1 clove garlic, crushed
375g uncooked king prawns, shelled
250g squid hoods, sliced
250g fresh egg noodles
2 tablespoons oil
4 green shallots, chopped
1 red pepper, sliced
230g can sliced bamboo
    shoots, drained

Combine honey, sauces, sherry, oil,
ginger, garlic, prawns and squid in bowl;
cover, refrigerate 3 hours or overnight.

Add noodles to large pan of boiling
water, boil, uncovered, until just tender;
drain, rinse under cold water; drain.

Remove seafood from marinade,
reserve marinade. Heat oil in wok or pan,
add shallots, pepper and bamboo shoots,
stir over heat for 1 minute; add seafood,
stir-fry until tender.

Stir in noodles and reserved marinade;
stir until mixture is heated through.
Remove from heat, cool; cover, refrigerate
for 2 hours before serving.

Serves 6.

■ Salad can be made a day ahead.
■ Storage: Covered, in refrigerator.
■ Freeze: Not suitable.
■ Microwave: Noodles suitable.

SMOKED TROUT WITH BUTTERED HERB PASTA

375g sliced smoked ocean trout
½ x 250g punnet cherry tomatoes
⅓ cup sliced black olives
1 teaspoon chopped fresh dill
1 tablespoon sugar
2 tablespoons lime juice
1½ teaspoons French mustard
⅓ cup olive oil

BUTTERED HERB PASTA
1½ cups plain flour
¼ cup fine semolina
¼ cup cornmeal
3 eggs
3 teaspoons chopped fresh mint
3 teaspoons chopped fresh dill
3 teaspoons chopped fresh basil
90g unsalted butter
1 tablespoon chopped fresh
    basil, extra
2 teaspoons chopped fresh
    mint, extra

Cut trout into thin strips, combine with
tomatoes, olives and dill in bowl. Pour
over combined sugar, juice, mustard and
oil; cover, refrigerate 2 hours, stirring
occasionally.

Serve trout mixture with warm pasta.

Buttered Herb Pasta: Process flour,
semolina, cornmeal, eggs and herbs until
mixture forms a ball; cover with plastic
wrap, stand 2 hours.

Knead dough until smooth, roll until
2mm thick, cut into thin strips using pasta
machine. Add pasta to large pan of boiling
water, boil, uncovered, for about 2

minutes or until just tender; drain.

Heat butter in pan, add extra herbs and pasta, stir gently until combined.

Serves 6.

■ Recipe can be prepared a day ahead.
■ Storage: Covered, in refrigerator.
■ Freeze: Not suitable.
■ Microwave: Pasta suitable.

CRAB AND NOODLE SALAD WITH LEMON DRESSING

300g fresh egg noodles
1 stick celery
1 apple, chopped
1 tablespoon lemon juice
1½ tablespoons chopped fresh dill
2 x 170g cans crab meat, drained, flaked

LEMON DRESSING
1 teaspoon French mustard
1 teaspoon sugar
1 tablespoon white vinegar
2 tablespoons lemon juice
2 tablespoons olive oil

Add noodles to large pan of boiling water, boil, uncovered, until just tender; drain. Rinse noodles under cold water; drain.

Cut celery into 5cm sticks. Combine celery, apple, juice, dill, crab, noodles and dressing in bowl; mix well.

Lemon Dressing: Combine all ingredients in jar; shake well.

Serves 6.

■ Salad can be made a day ahead.
■ Storage: Covered, in refrigerator.
■ Freeze: Not suitable.
■ Microwave: Noodles suitable.

LEFT: Five Seafoods with Fennel Cream Sauce.
ABOVE: Clockwise from front: Smoked Trout with Buttered Herb Pasta, Crab and Noodle Salad with Lemon Dressing, Stir-Fried Seafood Salad.

Left: Plate and fabric from Les Olivades. Above: Plates from Accoutrement

SMOKED SALMON WITH FRESH ASPARAGUS

500g spaghetti pasta
400g sliced smoked salmon
2 tablespoons olive oil
1 onion, chopped
2 bunches (24 spears) fresh asparagus, chopped
1 tablespoon brandy
2 teaspoons white mustard seeds
2 x 300ml cartons cream
2 tablespoons shredded fresh basil

Add pasta to large pan of boiling water, boil, uncovered, until just tender, drain.

Cut salmon into 2cm strips. Heat oil in pan, add onion, cook, stirring, until soft. Add salmon, asparagus, brandy, seeds and cream. Bring to boil, simmer, uncovered, until slightly thickened; stir in basil. Serve hot sauce over pasta.

Serves 4.

■ Recipe best made just before serving.
■ Freeze: Not suitable.
■ Microwave: Suitable.

LEFT: From back: Eggplant and Anchovy Pasta, Smoked Salmon with Fresh Asparagus.
BELOW: Spinach Fettucine with Prawns and Artichokes.

EGGPLANT AND ANCHOVY PASTA

375g penne pasta
1 medium (about 300g) eggplant
4 medium (about 400g) zucchini
2 tablespoons olive oil
1 clove garlic, crushed
1 small fresh red chilli, finely chopped
1 onion, chopped
56g can anchovy fillets, drained, chopped
60g butter

Add pasta to large pan of boiling water, boil, uncovered, until just tender, drain.

Cut eggplant and zucchini into 6cm strips. Heat oil in pan, add garlic, chilli and onion, cook, stirring, until onion is soft. Add eggplant and zucchini, cook, stirring, until tender. Stir in anchovies and butter, stir until butter is melted. Add pasta, stir until heated through.

Serves 4.

■ Recipe best made close to serving.
■ Freeze: Not suitable.
■ Microwave: Pasta suitable.

Below: Plate from Accoutrement

SPINACH FETTUCINE WITH PRAWNS AND ARTICHOKES

500g cooked king prawns
¼ cup olive oil
2 cloves garlic, crushed
1 small onion, chopped
1 red pepper, chopped
2 x 410g cans tomatoes
1 tablespoon chopped fresh chives
2 tablespoons chopped fresh basil
275g jar artichoke hearts, drained, halved
500g packet spinach fettucine pasta
100g feta cheese, crumbled

Shell and devein prawns, leaving tails intact. Heat oil in pan, add garlic, onion and pepper, cook, stirring, until onion and pepper are soft. Stir in undrained crushed tomatoes, bring to boil, simmer, uncovered, for about 5 minutes or until slightly thickened. Stir in herbs, artichokes and prawns, cook until heated through.

Add pasta to large pan of boiling water, boil, uncovered, until just tender; drain. Serve hot pasta with hot sauce, topped with cheese.

Serves 4.

■ Recipe best made close to serving.
■ Freeze: Not suitable.
■ Microwave: Pasta suitable.

CHEESY SALMON LASAGNE

30g butter
2 onions, chopped
1 clove garlic, crushed
1 stick celery, chopped
2 x 425g cans tomatoes
1 tablespoon tomato paste
440g can salmon, drained, flaked
240g packet instant lasagne
    pasta sheets
1 tablespoon grated parmesan
    cheese

CHEESE SAUCE
60g butter
¼ cup plain flour
1 cup milk
250g cottage cheese
½ cup grated tasty cheese
2 eggs, lightly beaten

Heat butter in pan, add onions, garlic and celery; cook, stirring, until onions are soft. Stir in undrained crushed tomatoes and paste, bring to boil, simmer, uncovered, for 15 minutes; stir in salmon.

Cover base of greased 20cm x 30cm ovenproof dish with a layer of pasta. Spread pasta with half the salmon mixture, then half the cheese sauce; repeat layers ending with cheese sauce; sprinkle with parmesan cheese. Bake lasagne in moderate oven for about 45 minutes or until lightly browned.

Cheese Sauce: Melt butter in pan, stir in flour, stir over heat until bubbling. Remove from heat, gradually stir in milk, stir over heat until sauce boils and thickens. Remove sauce from heat, stir in cheeses and eggs.

Serves 6.

■ Recipe can be made a day ahead.
■ Storage: Covered, in refrigerator.
■ Freeze: Not suitable.
■ Microwave: Not suitable.

ORANGE AND SALMON PASTA SALAD

250g farfalle pasta
2 teaspoons olive oil
250g Atlantic salmon cutlet
2 green shallots, chopped
2 oranges, segmented
1 stick celery, chopped
½ cup pecans
3 cups (250g) shredded red cabbage

DRESSING
¼ cup olive oil
1 tablespoon lemon juice
1 teaspoon light soy sauce
1 clove garlic, crushed

Add pasta to large pan of boiling water, boil, uncovered, until just tender; drain.

Combine pasta and oil in bowl. Add salmon to shallow pan of simmering water, simmer, covered, for about 5 minutes or until tender; cool. Remove skin and bones from salmon, break salmon into pieces.

Just before serving, combine pasta, salmon, shallots, oranges, celery, nuts and cabbage in bowl; mix well. Add dressing, toss lightly.

Dressing: Combine all ingredients in jar; shake well.

Serves 4.

■ Salad can be made 3 hours ahead.
■ Storage: Covered, in refrigerator.
■ Freeze: Not suitable.
■ Microwave: Suitable.

SALMON AND RISONI BONBONS

½ cup plain flour
2 teaspoons tomato paste
2 eggs, lightly beaten
¾ cup milk
16 long fresh chives
20g butter, melted
1 tablespoon chopped fresh chives
1 clove garlic, crushed

FILLING
½ cup risoni pasta
210g can salmon, drained, mashed
2 tablespoons horseradish cream
1 green shallot, finely chopped
2 tablespoons sour cream

Sift flour into bowl, gradually stir in combined paste, eggs and milk, beat until smooth (or blend or process all ingredients until smooth); cover, stand for 30 minutes.

Pour 2 to 3 tablespoons of batter into heated greased heavy-based crepe pan, cook until lightly browned underneath. Turn crepe, brown on other side. Repeat with remaining batter. You will need 8 crepes for this recipe.

Divide filling along 1 side of each crepe, roll crepes firmly. Drop long chives into pan of boiling water; drain. Tie a chive around each end of bonbons. Place bonbons on lightly greased oven tray, cover loosely with foil.

Just before serving, heat bonbons in moderate oven for about 10 minutes. Brush with combined butter, chopped chives and garlic.

Filling: Add pasta to pan of boiling water, boil, uncovered, until just tender; drain. Combine pasta, salmon, horseradish, shallot and sour cream in bowl.

Serves 4.

■ Bonbons can be made 2 days ahead.
■ Storage: Covered, in refrigerator.
■ Freeze: Unfilled crepes suitable.
■ Microwave: Pasta suitable.

LEFT: Salmon and Risoni Bonbons.
RIGHT: From back: Cheesy Salmon Lasagne, Orange and Salmon Pasta Salad.

SALMON CHUNKS IN CRISP CHAMPAGNE BATTER

150g capellini egg noodles
1½ bunches (18 spears) fresh
 asparagus
1 tablespoon olive oil
1 clove garlic, crushed
3 green shallots, chopped
1 tablespoon light soy sauce
300ml carton thickened cream
2 thick (600g) Atlantic salmon steaks
oil for deep-frying
¼ cup lemon juice

CHAMPAGNE BATTER
⅔ cup plain flour
⅓ cup champagne
⅓ cup soda water

Add noodles to large pan of boiling water, boil, uncovered, until just tender; drain. Cut asparagus into 3cm lengths. Heat olive oil in pan, add asparagus, garlic and shallots, cook, stirring, for 3 minutes. Remove from heat, stir in sauce. Bring cream to boil in separate pan, simmer, uncovered, for about 4 minutes or until thickened slightly, stir into asparagus mixture. Cut salmon into bite-sized chunks.
Just before serving, dip salmon chunks in batter, deep-fry in hot oil until lightly browned and crisp; drain on absorbent paper. Combine hot noodles and sauce, fold in salmon, sprinkle with juice.
Champagne Batter: Sift flour into bowl, stir in champagne and soda water all at once, beat to a smooth batter.
 Serves 4.

■ Recipe can be prepared 6 hours ahead. Batter best made just before using.
■ Storage: Covered, in refrigerator.
■ Freeze: Not suitable.
■ Microwave: Noodles suitable.

LOBSTER IN WINE AND PEPPERCORN GLAZE

2 lobster tails
plain flour
20g butter
1 tablespoon port
½ cup dry white wine
½ cup water
1 small chicken stock cube, crumbled
1 tablespoon canned drained
 green peppercorns
¼ cup cream
375g casarecce pasta
30g butter, extra
1 tablespoon chopped fresh parsley

Remove lobster meat from shells in 1 piece; cut meat into 1½cm medallions. Toss lobster in flour, shake away excess flour. Heat butter in pan, add medallions in single layer, cook about 2 minutes on each side or until almost tender. Add port, wine, water, stock cube and peppercorns, simmer gently, covered, until medallions are tender. Remove medallions from pan; keep warm.

Boil sauce, uncovered, for about 3 minutes or until reduced to a shiny glaze, add cream, stir until heated through.

Add pasta to large pan of boiling water, boil, uncovered, until just tender; drain. Add extra butter to same pan, stir until melted and lightly browned, return pasta to pan with parsley, mix well. Serve pasta with lobster and sauce.
 Serves 4.

■ Recipe best made just before serving.
■ Freeze: Not suitable.
■ Microwave: Pasta suitable.

ABOVE: From back: Salmon Chunks in Crisp Champagne Batter, Lobster in Wine and Peppercorn Glaze.

PRAWN AND CRAB CASSEROLE

125g ziti pasta
50g butter
⅓ cup grated fresh parmesan cheese

FILLING
80g butter
⅓ cup plain flour
1½ cups milk
1 cup (80g) grated fresh
    parmesan cheese
80g cooked shelled prawns, chopped
170g can crab meat, drained, flaked
1 tablespoon chopped fresh chives
5 eggs, separated

Lightly grease 6cm deep ovenproof dish (8 cup capacity). Add pasta to large pan of boiling water, boil, uncovered, until just tender; drain. Return pasta to pan, stir butter and cheese through pasta; cool.

Cut pasta into 5cm lengths, stand pasta around edge of prepared dish. Chop remaining pasta, combine with filling. Pour filling into dish, bake in moderately hot oven for about 35 minutes or until set and well browned.

Filling: Melt butter in pan, stir in flour, stir over heat until bubbling. Remove from heat, gradually stir in milk, stir over heat until sauce boils and thickens; cool 5 minutes. Stir in cheese, prawns, crab, chives and lightly beaten egg yolks. Beat egg whites in small bowl with electric mixer until soft peaks form, fold lightly into prawn mixture.

Serves 6.

■ Recipe best made close to serving.
■ Freeze: Not suitable.
■ Microwave: Pasta suitable.

CRISPY FISH WITH LEEK AND NOODLES

¼ cup cornflour
¼ teaspoon five spice powder
1 egg, lightly beaten
1 teaspoon dark soy sauce
500g white fish fillets
6 Chinese dried mushrooms
40g butter
2 teaspoons grated fresh ginger
1 leek, thinly sliced
¼ cup roasted unsalted cashews
¼ cup oyster sauce
250g fresh egg noodles
2 teaspoons sesame oil
1 tablespoon chopped fresh coriander
oil for deep-frying
2 green shallots, sliced

Sift cornflour and spice into bowl, stir in egg and soy sauce, stir until smooth. Chop fish into 2cm cubes, add to cornflour mixture, mix well; cover, refrigerate 1 hour.

Place mushrooms in bowl, cover with boiling water, stand 20 minutes. Drain mushrooms, discard liquid. Discard stems, slice caps thinly.

Melt butter in pan, add ginger and leek, cook, stirring, until leek is soft. Remove from heat, stir in cashews, oyster sauce and mushrooms; keep warm.

Place noodles in heatproof bowl, cover with boiling water, stand 5 minutes; drain. Add noodles to leek mixture, stir in sesame oil and coriander; heat through.

Deep-fry fish pieces in batches in hot oil until well browned and cooked through; drain on absorbent paper. Serve fish over noodle mixture, sprinkle with shallots.

Serves 4.

■ Fish can be prepared a day ahead.
■ Storage: Covered, in refrigerator.
■ Freeze: Not suitable.
■ Microwave: Not suitable.

BELOW: From left: Crispy Fish with Leek and Noodles, Prawn and Crab Casserole.
Plate and tiles from Country Floors

BEEF

Expect the unexpected in this section, because we've been generous with assertive flavours to enhance the good robust taste of beef, so satisfyingly partnered by pasta.
Just to tempt you, there are tender cuts of steak and pastrami to serve in smart salads, in stir-fries with noodles, a curry or double-fried into crisp, spicy morsels. And there's mince, lots of mince, terrifically tasty in just over half the recipes.

WARM BEEF AND WALNUT SALAD

500g pasta elbows
500g piece beef eye-fillet
2 tablespoons lemon juice
2 tablespoons light soy sauce
1 tablespoon oyster sauce
2 cloves garlic, crushed
2 tablespoons olive oil
1 red pepper, chopped
1 cup (120g) chopped walnuts
4 green shallots, chopped

DRESSING
¼ cup olive oil
1 clove garlic, crushed
1 tablespoon white vinegar
1 tablespoon lemon juice
1 tablespoon chopped fresh chives

Add pasta to large pan of boiling water, boil, uncovered, until just tender, drain; keep warm.

Cut beef into 1cm cubes, combine with juice, sauces and garlic in bowl; cover, refrigerate 1 hour.

Heat oil in pan, add beef mixture in batches, cook, stirring, until beef is cooked as desired. Combine beef mixture and pasta in bowl; keep warm.

Add pepper to pan of boiling water, boil 1 minute; drain. Add pepper, nuts, shallots and dressing to pasta; toss well.
Dressing: Combine all ingredients in pan, stir over heat until heated through.
Serves 4.

■ Recipe best made just before serving.
■ Freeze: Not suitable.
■ Microwave: Pasta suitable.

PARSLEY MINCEBALLS IN CREAMY CHEESE SAUCE

500g minced beef
1 onion, finely chopped
1 egg, lightly beaten
¼ cup tomato paste
1 tablespoon Worcestershire sauce
¼ cup chopped fresh parsley
1 cup (70g) stale breadcrumbs
plain flour
oil for deep-frying
375g tagliatelle pasta
60g butter
300ml carton cream
2 cups (160g) grated fresh
    parmesan cheese
¼ cup chopped fresh parsley, extra

Combine mince, onion, egg, paste, sauce, parsley and breadcrumbs in bowl; mix well. Shape 3 level teaspoons into a ball, toss lightly in flour; shake off excess flour. Repeat with remaining mixture.

Deep-fry meatballs in hot oil until well browned and cooked through, drain on absorbent paper; keep warm.

Add pasta to large pan of boiling water, boil, uncovered, until just tender; drain.

Melt butter in pan, stir in cream and cheese, stir, without boiling, until sauce is heated through. Remove sauce from heat, stir in extra parsley and meatballs, serve over pasta.
Serves 4.

■ Meatballs can be made a day ahead. Sauce best made close to serving.
■ Storage: Covered, in refrigerator.
■ Freeze: Meatballs suitable.
■ Microwave: Pasta suitable.

EASY BEEF RAVIOLI WITH LEMON DRESSING

500g beef ravioli
100g mushrooms, sliced
390g can pimientos, drained, sliced
⅓ cup black olives, sliced
⅓ cup small fresh oregano leaves

LEMON DRESSING
⅓ cup lemon juice
½ cup olive oil
1 clove garlic, crushed
½ teaspoon sugar
¼ teaspoon seasoned pepper

Add ravioli to large pan of boiling water, boil, uncovered, until just tender; drain.

Combine ravioli, mushrooms, pimientos, olives and oregano in bowl; mix well. Pour over dressing; mix well.
Dressing: Combine all ingredients in jar; shake well.
Serves 4.

■ Can be made several hours ahead.
■ Storage: Covered, in refrigerator.
■ Freeze: Not suitable.
■ Microwave: Not suitable.

RIGHT: Clockwise from front: Warm Beef and Walnut Salad, Easy Beef Ravioli with Lemon Dressing, Parsley Minceballs in Creamy Cheese Sauce.
Plates from Home and Garden

SPICY BEEF PIE WITH TOMATO SALSA

125g spaghettini pasta
2 eggs, lightly beaten
½ cup sour cream
1 cup (80g) grated fresh
    parmesan cheese
1 tablespoon olive oil
1 onion, finely chopped
250g minced beef
35g sachet chilli seasoning mix
1 tablespoon tomato paste
1 cup water
1 small chicken stock cube, crumbled
439g can garbanzos, rinsed, drained

TOMATO SALSA
2 large tomatoes, finely chopped
2 green shallots, chopped
½ teaspoon sugar
1 tablespoon lemon juice
1 tablespoon chopped fresh coriander

Add pasta to large pan of boiling water, boil, uncovered, until just tender; drain.

Combine pasta, eggs, sour cream and half the cheese in bowl. Heat oil in pan, add onion, cook, stirring, until soft. Add mince, cook, stirring, until well browned. Stir in seasoning mix, paste, water and stock cube. Bring to boil, simmer, uncovered, for 5 minutes. Stir in garbanzos, simmer, uncovered, further 5 minutes or until thickened.

Press half the pasta mixture over base and side of greased 23cm pie dish. Spread with mince mixture, press firmly. Top with remaining pasta mixture, sprinkle with remaining cheese. Bake pie in moderate oven for about 1¼ hours or until well browned. Stand pie 5 minutes before cutting, serve with tomato salsa.

Tomato Salsa: Combine all ingredients in bowl; cover, stand 20 minutes.

Serves 6.

■ Recipe can be made a day ahead.
■ Storage: Covered, in refrigerator.
■ Freeze: Pie suitable.
■ Microwave: Pasta suitable.

TWO-MINCE MEATBALLS IN STROGANOFF SAUCE

250g minced beef
250g sausage mince
1 egg, lightly beaten
1 cup (70g) stale breadcrumbs
¼ cup tomato paste
60g butter
2 onions, sliced
2 cloves garlic, crushed
2 tablespoons plain flour
2 cups water
1 small chicken stock cube, crumbled
¼ cup dry red wine
500g fettucine pasta
250g mushrooms, chopped
¼ cup sour cream
1 tablespoon chopped fresh parsley

Combine minces, egg, breadcrumbs and paste in bowl; mix well. Shape 1 level tablespoon of mixture into a ball; repeat with remaining mixture.

Melt butter in pan, add meatballs in single layer, cook, shaking pan occasionally, until browned and cooked through; drain on absorbent paper.

Drain pan, leaving 2 tablespoons drippings in pan. Add onions and garlic to pan, cook, stirring, until onions are soft. Stir in flour, stir over heat until bubbling. Remove from heat, gradually stir in combined water, stock cube and wine, stir over heat until mixture boils and thickens.

Add pasta to large pan of boiling water, boil, uncovered, until just tender; drain.

Just before serving, combine mushrooms, sour cream, parsley and meatballs in pan, stir over heat until heated through, serve with pasta.

Serves 4.

■ Recipe can be made a day ahead.
■ Storage: Covered, in refrigerator.
■ Freeze: Cooked meatballs suitable.
■ Microwave: Pasta suitable.

PASTRAMI AND DILL SALAD

3 cups (240g) curled frilly pasta
100g green beans, sliced
200g sliced pastrami, chopped
3 gherkins, sliced
½ x 250g punnet cherry tomatoes

DRESSING
300g carton sour cream
1 teaspoon grated orange rind
½ cup orange juice
¼ cup lemon juice
3 teaspoons seeded mustard
1 teaspoon chopped fresh dill

Add pasta to large pan of boiling water, boil, uncovered, until just tender; drain. Rinse pasta under cold water; drain well.

Boil, steam or microwave beans until tender, rinse under cold water; drain. Combine pasta, beans, pastrami, gherkins and tomatoes in bowl, add dressing; toss well.

Dressing: Combine all ingredients in bowl; mix well.

Serves 6.

■ Salad can be made 6 hours ahead.
■ Storage: Covered, in refrigerator.
■ Freeze: Not suitable.
■ Microwave: Suitable.

LEFT: From left: Pastrami and Dill Salad, Two-Mince Meatballs in Stroganoff Sauce, Spicy Beef Pie with Tomato Salsa.

quarters between filling and trim edges using a pastry cutter. Repeat with remaining wrappers, egg white and filling.

Just before serving, add ravioli to large pan of boiling water, boil, uncovered, for about 4 minutes or until just tender; drain. Serve ravioli with teriyaki sauce.

Teriyaki Sauce: Melt 40g of the butter in pan, stir in flour, stir over heat until bubbling. Remove from heat, gradually stir in combined water, marinade, wine and remaining butter. Stir over high heat until sauce boils and thickens, stir in pepper and shallots, simmer 1 minute.

Serves 4.

■ Ravioli and sauce can be prepared 3 hours ahead.
■ Storage: Covered, in refrigerator.
■ Freeze: Uncooked ravioli suitable.
■ Microwave: Sauce suitable.

BEEF CURRY WITH YOGURT AND COCONUT CREAM

¼ **cup olive oil**
2 **onions, sliced**
1kg **chuck steak, chopped**
2 **cloves garlic, crushed**
½ **teaspoon ground cardamom**
1 **teaspoon ground cinnamon**
1 **teaspoon garam masala**
1 **tablespoon hot chilli sauce**
1 **tablespoon sugar**
150g **can coconut cream**
200g **carton plain yogurt**
1 **cup water**
2 **tablespoons lemon juice**
2 **small green cucumbers, sliced**
375g **fusilli pasta**
1 **teaspoon cumin seeds**
2 **tablespoons chopped fresh coriander**

Heat oil in pan, add onions, cook, stirring, until soft. Add steak, cook, stirring, until well browned. Stir in garlic, spices, sauce, sugar, coconut cream, yogurt and water. Bring to boil, simmer, covered, for about 1 hour or until steak is tender, stirring occasionally.

Remove cover, simmer, further 15 minutes or until slightly thickened. Stir in juice and cucumbers, remove from heat, stand covered, for 5 minutes.

Add pasta to large pan of boiling water, boil, uncovered, until just tender; drain. Combine pasta with seeds and coriander, serve with curry.

Serves 6.

■ Curry can be made a day ahead.
■ Storage: Covered, in refrigerator.
■ Freeze: Curry suitable.
■ Microwave: Pasta suitable.

SPICY BEEF AND PASTA CASSEROLE

500g **wholemeal pasta wheels**
2 **tablespoons olive oil**
1 **tablespoon bottled chopped chillies**
2 **cloves garlic, crushed**
2 **(about 240g) red Spanish onions, sliced**
750g **minced beef**
390g **can pimientos, drained, chopped**
2 x 410g **cans tomatoes**
440g **can corn kernels, drained**
½ **teaspoon cracked black peppercorns**
250g **mozzarella cheese, grated**

Add pasta to large pan of boiling water, boil, uncovered, until just tender; drain.

Heat oil in pan, add chillies, garlic and onions, cook, stirring, until onions are soft. Add mince, cook, stirring, until well browned. Stir in pimientos, undrained crushed tomatoes, corn and peppercorns.

Spoon half the pasta into greased ovenproof dish (12 cup capacity). Top with half the mince mixture and half the cheese, continue layering, finishing with cheese. Bake, uncovered, in moderate oven for about 15 minutes or until heated through and cheese is melted.

Serves 8.

■ Recipe can be made a day ahead.
■ Storage: Covered, in refrigerator.
■ Freeze: Suitable.
■ Microwave: Pasta suitable.

BEEF AND BACON RAVIOLI WITH TERIYAKI SAUCE

125g **minced beef**
1 **small onion, chopped**
1 **bacon rasher, chopped**
1 **clove garlic, crushed**
1 **tablespoon chopped fresh parsley**
¼ **teaspoon ground nutmeg**
250g **packet wonton wrappers**
1 **egg white, lightly beaten**

TERIYAKI SAUCE
100g **unsalted butter**
2 **tablespoons plain flour**
1 **cup water**
¼ **cup teriyaki marinade**
⅓ **cup green ginger wine**
½ **red pepper, thinly sliced**
2 **green shallots, sliced**

Blend or process mince, onion, bacon, garlic, parsley and nutmeg until smooth. Brush a wonton wrapper lightly with egg white, place ½ level teaspoon of filling in each quarter of wrapper. Top with a second wrapper, press between filling and on edges of wrappers to seal. Cut into

ABOVE LEFT: Spicy Beef and Pasta Casserole.
RIGHT: From left: Beef Curry with Yogurt and Coconut Cream, Beef and Bacon Ravioli with Teriyaki Sauce.
Right: Plates from Villa Italiana

CHEESY SPAGHETTI AND MINCE SLICE

125g butter
1 cup plain flour
1 litre (4 cups) milk
3 egg yolks
1¾ cups (150g) finely grated
    kefalogravier (sheep's milk) cheese
500g spaghetti pasta
90g butter, extra
¼ cup stale breadcrumbs
¼ teaspoon ground nutmeg

MEAT SAUCE
60g butter
2 onions, chopped
1 clove garlic, crushed
1kg minced beef
4 large (about 660g) tomatoes,
    peeled, chopped
1 tablespoon tomato paste
2 teaspoons sugar
4 whole cloves
1 bay leaf
¼ teaspoon ground cinnamon
3 egg whites

Melt butter in pan, add flour, stir over heat until bubbling. Remove from heat, gradually stir in milk, stir over heat until mixture boils and thickens. Stir in egg yolks and ⅓ cup of the cheese; cool.

Add pasta to large pan of boiling water, boil, uncovered, until just tender; drain; cool. Melt extra butter in same pan until lightly browned, stir in pasta, remove from heat. Stir in 1⅓ cups of remaining cheese, stir until well combined.

Spread half the pasta mixture into greased 27cm x 33cm baking dish. Top with half the meat sauce, then remaining pasta mixture, spread with remaining meat sauce. Top with cheese sauce, sprinkle with combined breadcrumbs, nutmeg and remaining cheese. Bake in moderate oven for about 40 minutes or until lightly browned.

Meat Sauce: Heat butter in pan, add onions and garlic, cook, stirring, until onions are soft. Add mince, cook, stirring, until well browned. Stir in tomatoes, paste, sugar, cloves, bay leaf and cinnamon, bring to boil, simmer, uncovered, for 20 minutes. Remove cloves and bay leaf; cool. Stir in lightly beaten egg whites.

Serves 8.

■ Slice best made a day ahead.
■ Storage: Covered, in refrigerator.
■ Freeze: Suitable.
■ Microwave: Pasta suitable.

EASY PASTRAMI AND PIMIENTO STIR-FRY

⅓ cup olive oil
2 onions, sliced
2 cloves garlic, crushed
250g casarecce pasta
390g can pimientos, drained, sliced
100g pastrami, sliced
2 tablespoons chopped fresh parsley

Heat oil in pan, add onions and garlic, cook, stirring, until onions are soft.

Add pasta to large pan of boiling water, boil, uncovered, until just tender; drain.

Add pasta, pimientos, pastrami and parsley to onion mixture, stir until heated through.

Serves 4.

■ Recipe best made just before serving.
■ Freeze: Not suitable.
■ Microwave: Pasta suitable.

RIGHT: From left: Cheesy Spaghetti and Mince Slice, Easy Pastrami and Pimiento Stir-Fry.

Plates from Country Floors

HERBED MEATBALL BAKE WITH CREAMY BACON SAUCE

500g rigatoni pasta
⅓ cup grated fresh parmesan cheese

MEATBALLS
1 slice white bread, chopped
¼ cup milk
750g minced beef
1 onion, grated
1 clove garlic, crushed
¼ cup grated fresh parmesan cheese
2 tablespoons chopped fresh parsley
2 tablespoons chopped fresh basil
oil for shallow-frying

SAUCE
3 bacon rashers, chopped
125g butter
½ cup plain flour
1¼ litres (5 cups) milk
¼ cup dry white wine
1½ tablespoons seeded mustard
2 tablespoons chopped fresh chives

Add pasta to large pan of boiling water, boil, uncovered, until just tender; drain.

Combine pasta and meatballs in greased ovenproof dish (10 cup capacity). Top with sauce, sprinkle with cheese. Bake, uncovered, in moderate oven for about 15 minutes or until heated through.
Meatballs: Combine bread and milk in bowl; stand 5 minutes. Combine bread mixture, mince, onion, garlic, cheese and herbs in bowl; mix well. Roll 2 tablespoons of mixture into a ball, repeat with remaining mixture.

Shallow-fry meatballs in hot oil until well browned and cooked through; drain on absorbent paper.
Sauce: Add bacon to pan, cook, stirring, until crisp; remove from pan. Melt butter in pan, add flour, stir over heat until bubbling. Remove from heat, stir in milk and wine, stir over heat until sauce boils and thickens. Stir in mustard, chives and bacon.

Serves 6.

■ Recipe can be made a day head.
■ Storage: Covered, in refrigerator.
■ Freeze: Not suitable.
■ Microwave: Pasta suitable.

TASTY MINCE AND SPAGHETTI CASSEROLE

250g packet spinach spaghetti pasta
1 tablespoon olive oil
1 onion, finely chopped
1 clove garlic, crushed
500g minced beef
425g can tomato puree
125g mushrooms, sliced
2 tablespoons chopped fresh parsley
2 teaspoons sugar
½ cup grated fresh parmesan cheese

SAUCE
30g butter
2 tablespoons plain flour
1½ cups milk

Add pasta to large pan of boiling water, boil, uncovered, until just tender; drain.

Heat oil in pan, add onion and garlic, cook, stirring, until onion is soft. Add mince, cook, stirring, until browned. Stir in puree, bring to boil, simmer, covered, 15 minutes. Stir in mushrooms, parsley and sugar, simmer, uncovered, further 5 minutes.

Spread half the pasta into greased ovenproof dish (8 cup capacity). Top with mince mixture, then remaining pasta, pour over sauce; sprinkle with cheese. Bake in a moderately hot oven for about 15 minutes or until lightly browned.
Sauce: Melt butter in pan, add flour, stir over heat until bubbling. Remove from heat, gradually stir in milk, stir over heat until sauce boils and thickens.

Serves 4.

■ Recipe can be made a day ahead.
■ Storage: Covered, in refrigerator.
■ Freeze: Suitable.
■ Microwave: Pasta suitable.

RUMP STEAK WITH BRANDIED BLUE CHEESE SAUCE

500g rump steak
1 tablespoon olive oil
500g spinach fettucine pasta
1 green shallot, thinly sliced

SAUCE
40g butter
1 onion, chopped
2 tablespoons plain flour
1 cup water
1 small chicken stock cube, crumbled
½ cup milk
200g blue cheese, crumbled
1 tablespoon brandy
1 clove garlic, crushed

Cut steak into 5cm pieces. Heat oil in pan, add steak, cook over high heat until well browned and done as desired. Remove from heat; keep warm.

Just before serving, cut steak into thin strips. Add pasta to large pan of boiling water, boil, uncovered, until just tender; drain. Combine pasta, sauce and steak, top with shallot.
Sauce: Melt butter in pan, add onion, cook, stirring, until soft. Add flour, stir until bubbling. Remove from heat, gradually stir in combined water, stock cube and milk. Stir over heat until mixture boils and thickens, simmer, uncovered, for 3 minutes; cool slightly.

Blend or process sauce, cheese, brandy and garlic until smooth.

Serves 6.

■ Recipe best made just before serving.
■ Freeze: Not suitable.
■ Microwave: Pasta suitable.

LEFT: Clockwise from back: Rump Steak with Brandied Blue Cheese Sauce, Tasty Mince and Spaghetti Casserole, Herbed Meatball Bake with Creamy Bacon Sauce.

Rug from Janet Niven

CORIANDER MEATBALLS WITH GINGER PLUM SAUCE

1 tablespoon oil
1 onion, chopped
1 clove garlic, crushed
500g minced beef
1 cup (70g) stale breadcrumbs
1 egg, lightly beaten
2 teaspoons chopped fresh coriander
oil for deep-frying
200g fresh egg noodles

SAUCE
6 Chinese dried mushrooms
5cm piece fresh ginger
1 tablespoon olive oil
1 onion, thinly sliced
1 clove garlic, crushed
¼ cup dry sherry
2½ cups water
1 small chicken stock cube, crumbled
¼ cup plum sauce
125g snow peas
2 green shallots, chopped
1 tablespoon cornflour
2 tablespoons water, extra

Heat oil in pan, add onion and garlic, cook, stirring, until onion is soft. Combine mince, breadcrumbs, egg, coriander and onion mixture in bowl; mix well. Shape level tablespoons of mixture into balls using floured hands, place on tray; cover, refrigerate 1 hour.

Deep-fry meatballs in hot oil until well browned and cooked through; drain on absorbent paper. Add meatballs to sauce, keep warm.

Add noodles to large pan of boiling water, boil, uncovered, until just tender; drain; serve with meatballs and sauce.

Sauce: Place mushrooms in bowl, cover with boiling water, stand 20 minutes. Drain mushrooms. Discard stems, slice caps thinly. Cut ginger into thin strips.

Heat oil in pan, add onion, garlic and ginger, cook, stirring, until onion is soft. Add sherry, bring to boil, simmer, uncovered, for 1 minute. Stir in combined water, stock cube and sauce, bring to boil, simmer, uncovered, for 15 minutes. Add mushrooms, peas and shallots to pan, simmer 1 minute. Stir in blended cornflour and extra water, stir over heat until sauce boils and thickens.

Serves 4.

■ Meatballs and sauce can be made a day ahead.
■ Storage: Covered, in refrigerator.
■ Freeze: Cooked meatballs suitable.
■ Microwave: Noodles suitable.

HOT PASTRAMI AND ARTICHOKE SALAD

600g sliced pastrami
¼ cup olive oil
2 x 400g cans artichoke hearts, drained, quartered
⅓ cup sugar
1¼ cups dry red wine
1 red pepper, sliced
½ cup black olives
¼ cup shredded fresh basil leaves
300g rigatoni pasta
15 small fresh basil leaves, extra

Cut pastrami into thin strips. Heat oil in pan, add artichokes, cook, stirring, until lightly browned. Add pastrami, sugar and wine, bring to boil, simmer, uncovered, for 3 minutes. Add pepper, olives and shredded basil; cook 2 minutes.

Add pasta to large pan of boiling water, boil, uncovered, until just tender; drain.

Combine pasta with pastrami mixture and extra basil leaves.

Serves 4.

■ Recipe best made close to serving.
■ Freeze: Not suitable.
■ Microwave: Pasta suitable.

QUICK AND EASY LASAGNE

1 tablespoon olive oil
1 onion, finely chopped
1 clove garlic, crushed
500g minced beef
2 x 500g jars pasta sauce
240g packet (16) instant lasagne
   pasta sheets
500g ricotta cheese
½ cup milk
250g mozzarella cheese, grated
½ cup cream
¼ cup grated fresh parmesan cheese

Heat oil in pan, add onion and garlic, cook, stirring, until onion is soft. Add mince, cook, stirring, until well browned. Stir in pasta sauce, cook until heated through; remove from heat.

Line shallow greased 20cm x 30cm ovenproof dish with a layer of pasta, top with one-third of meat mixture. Spread with one-third of combined ricotta cheese and milk, sprinkle with one-third of mozzarella cheese. Repeat layering, finishing with pasta; pour over cream, sprinkle with parmesan cheese.

Bake in moderate oven for about 40 minutes or until pasta is tender. Cover lasagne with foil during cooking if surface begins to brown too quickly.

Serves 6.

■ Recipe can be made 2 days ahead.
■ Storage: Covered, in refrigerator.
■ Freeze: Not suitable.
■ Microwave: Not suitable.

LEFT: Coriander Meatballs with Ginger Plum Sauce.
BELOW: From back: Quick and Easy Lasagne, Hot Pastrami and Artichoke Salad.

Left: Plate from Accoutrement

CHEESE-TOPPED BEEF AND EGGPLANT BAKE

2 (about 800g) eggplants
salt
3 cups (200g) shell pasta
¼ cup olive oil
1 onion, chopped
2 cloves garlic, crushed
3 tomatoes, chopped
⅓ cup tomato paste
1½ cups water
2 teaspoons sugar
3 (about 300g) zucchini, chopped
1 large red pepper, chopped
500g piece beef eye-fillet, sliced
1 teaspoon dried tarragon leaves
2 cups (200g) grated
   mozzarella cheese
2 tablespoons chopped fresh parsley

Cut eggplants into 1cm slices, place on wire rack, sprinkle with salt, stand 30 minutes. Rinse eggplant under cold water, drain on absorbent paper.

Add pasta to large pan of boiling water, boil, uncovered, until just tender; drain.

Heat oil in pan, add onion and garlic, cook, stirring, until onion is soft. Stir in tomatoes, paste, water and sugar, bring to boil, simmer, uncovered, for 10 minutes. Stir in zucchini, pepper, beef and tarragon, simmer further 15 minutes. Stir in pasta, simmer, uncovered, until mixture is slightly thickened.

Spread one-third of beef mixture into greased ovenproof dish (10 cup capacity), top with a layer of eggplant. Repeat layering, finishing with eggplant.

Just before serving, sprinkle with cheese, bake in moderate oven for about 25 minutes or until eggplant is tender and cheese is lightly browned. Serve sprinkled with parsley.

  Serves 6.

■ Recipe can be prepared a day ahead.
■ Storage: Covered, in refrigerator.
■ Freeze: Not suitable.
■ Microwave: Pasta suitable.

DOUBLE-FRIED SHREDDED BEEF WITH TAGLIATELLE

750g piece rump steak
⅓ cup cornflour
2 tablespoons dark soy sauce
1 tablespoon oil
1 teaspoon five spice powder
½ teaspoon chilli powder
½ teaspoon ground ginger
2 carrots
oil for deep-frying
250g tagliatelle pasta
2 green shallots, sliced
30g butter

Remove excess fat from steak; wrap steak in plastic wrap, freeze for about 30 minutes or until partially frozen. Slice steak thinly, cut slices into fine shreds. Combine steak, cornflour, sauce, oil and spices in bowl; cover, refrigerate 1 hour.

Thinly slice carrots lengthways, cut into fine strips.

Deep-fry steak mixture in hot oil in several batches until lightly browned and crisp, stirring to separate steak; drain on absorbent paper.

Just before serving, add pasta to large pan of boiling water, boil, uncovered, until just tender; drain. Return pasta to pan, stir in shallots and butter; keep warm.

Reheat oil, deep-fry steak and carrots until steak is well browned; drain on absorbent paper. Serve steak and carrots over pasta mixture.

  Serves 4.

■ Steak can be prepared a day ahead. Deep-frying can begin 1 hour ahead.
■ Storage: Covered, in refrigerator.
■ Freeze. Not suitable.
■ Microwave: Pasta suitable.

LEFT: From left: Double-Fried Shredded Beef with Tagliatelle, Cheese-Topped Beef and Eggplant Bake.

Pottery from Something Special

STIR-FRIED CHILLI GARLIC STEAK WITH POTATOES

1 onion, chopped
4 cloves garlic, crushed
1½ teaspoons dried chilli flakes
1 tablespoon sugar
½ teaspoon dried shrimp paste
4 baby potatoes
2 tomatoes, peeled
2 tablespoons oil
500g rump steak, thinly sliced
6 green shallots, chopped
3 cups (240g) shredded
   Chinese cabbage
125g bean sprouts
375g packet fresh egg noodles
2 tablespoons light soy sauce
1 tablespoon sweet chilli sauce

Blend or process onion, garlic, chilli flakes, sugar and paste until smooth.

Boil, steam or microwave potatoes until just tender; cut into quarters. Cut tomatoes into wedges.

Heat half the oil in wok or pan, add onion mixture, stir-fry for 2 minutes. Add steak to wok in batches, stir-fry until well browned and tender; remove from pan.

Heat remaining oil in wok, add shallots, cabbage, sprouts and tomatoes, stir-fry until cabbage is wilted. Return steak to wok with noodles, stir in sauces, stir-fry until heated through. Serve with potatoes.

Serves 4.

■ Recipe best made close to serving.
■ Freeze: Not suitable.
■ Microwave: Potatoes suitable.

COOL 'N' SPICY BEEF WITH PASTA

200g pipe rigate pasta
1 tablespoon olive oil
500g minced beef
1 teaspoon ground coriander
1 teaspoon ground cumin
½ teaspoon ground cardamom
½ teaspoon garam masala
1 large red pepper
150g snow peas, chopped
5 green shallots, chopped
2 teaspoons chopped fresh coriander
¾ cup dates, sliced

Just before serving, stir in fresh coriander, dates and dressing; mix well.
Dressing: Combine all ingredients in jar; shake well.

Serves 6.

■ Salad can be made a day ahead. Dressing can be made 3 days ahead.
■ Storage: Covered, in refrigerator.
■ Freeze: Not suitable.
■ Microwave: Pasta suitable.

BEST EVER BOLOGNAISE SAUCE

1 tablespoon olive oil
2 onions, chopped
1 clove garlic, crushed
1kg minced beef
2 x 410g cans tomatoes
1½ cups water
½ cup dry white wine
2 tablespoons tomato paste
3 small beef stock cubes, crumbled
1 teaspoon dried oregano leaves
½ teaspoon dried marjoram leaves
½ teaspoon sugar

Heat oil in pan, add onions and garlic, cook, stirring, over low heat for about 15 minutes or until onions are very soft. Add mince, cook, stirring, until well browned. Stir in undrained crushed tomatoes, water, wine, paste, stock cubes, herbs and sugar. Bring to boil, simmer, uncovered, for about 2 hours or until sauce is thickened; stirring occasionally. Serve with pasta and grated parmesan cheese, if desired.

Serves 4.

■ Bolognaise sauce can be made 2 days ahead.
■ Storage: Covered, in refrigerator.
■ Freeze: Suitable.
■ Microwave: Not suitable.

LEFT: From left: Stir-Fried Chilli Garlic Steak with Potatoes, Cool 'n' Spicy Beef with Pasta. BELOW: Best Ever Bolognaise Sauce.

Below: Serving ware from Country Floors

DRESSING
2 tablespoons light soy sauce
¼ cup dry sherry
1 tablespoon mirin
2 teaspoons sugar
2 teaspoons sesame oil
2 teaspoons grated fresh ginger

Add pasta to large pan of boiling water, boil, uncovered, until just tender; drain.

Heat oil in pan, add mince and ground spices, cook, stirring, until well browned and tender; cool.

Quarter pepper, remove seeds and membrane. Grill pepper, skin side up, until skin blisters and blackens. Remove skin, chop pepper. Combine mince mixture, pepper, snow peas, shallots and pasta in bowl; cover, refrigerate.

LAMB

It's deliciously easy to serve lamb in tempting new ways when you add plenty of pasta, and these recipes abound in the unusual. For example, there's our cheesy, creamy torte or the clever coil of pasta with a hearty filling. Then there's green pea ravioli with minted lamb salad, honeyed lamb with noodles, and a quick chilli garlic lamb and noodle stir-fry. Favourites with a difference include lasagne, cannelloni, and, of course, roast lamb, only this time with pasta and a thick tomato sauce.

HONEYED LAMB WITH NOODLES AND OMELETTE

375g fresh egg noodles
800g lamb fillets
cornflour
oil for deep-frying
½ teaspoon ground ginger
¼ cup honey
½ cup lemon juice
½ cup water
2 teaspoons cornflour, extra
1 tablespoon light soy sauce
2 green shallots, sliced

OMELETTE
1 tablespoon milk
1 egg
1 teaspoon oil

Add noodles to large pan of boiling water, boil, uncovered, for about 5 minutes or until just tender, drain; keep warm.

Cut each lamb fillet into 4cm pieces, pound each piece until thin. Toss lamb in cornflour, shake away excess cornflour. Deep-fry lamb in hot oil until well browned and tender; drain on absorbent paper.

Combine ginger, honey, juice and water in pan, stir in blended extra cornflour and sauce. Stir over heat until sauce boils and thickens. Add lamb, stir until heated through, add shallots. Serve honeyed lamb over noodles, top with omelette.

Omelette: Beat milk and egg in bowl. Heat oil in large pan, add egg mixture, cook for about 3 minutes or until set; cool. Roll omelette tightly, slice finely.

Serves 4.

■ Recipe best made close to serving.
■ Freeze: Not suitable.
■ Microwave: Noodles suitable.

CREAMY LAMB AND CHICKEN PASTA COIL

500g packet ziti pasta
150g mushrooms, chopped
1⅓ cups (200g) chopped cooked chicken
18 black olives, halved
2 tablespoons chopped fresh basil

WHITE SAUCE
125g butter
½ cup plain flour
2 cups milk
¾ cup grated tasty cheese

LAMB SAUCE
1 tablespoon olive oil
1 onion, finely chopped
2 cloves garlic, crushed
500g minced lamb
410g can tomatoes
2 tablespoons tomato paste
2 tablespoons chopped fresh basil

Add pasta to large pan of boiling water, boil, uncovered, for three-quarters the recommended cooking time on packet; drain. Make white sauce and lamb sauce.

Line lightly greased ovenproof bowl (14 cup capacity) by coiling with half the pasta. Cut half the remaining pasta into 5cm lengths; reserve uncut pasta.

Spread one-third of the warm white sauce evenly over pasta in bowl, place one-third of meat sauce into bowl, top with half the chopped pasta.

Spread a little more white sauce over pasta. Top with half each of the mushrooms, chicken, olives and basil, half the remaining lamb sauce, then remaining chopped pasta.

Spread chopped pasta with half the remaining white sauce, top with remaining mushrooms, chicken, olives and basil. Spread with remaining lamb sauce.

Finish by coiling reserved uncut pasta over lamb sauce, spread with remaining white sauce.

Cover bowl with greased paper, then foil, place bowl in baking dish, pour in enough boiling water to come halfway up side of bowl. Bake in moderate oven for 45 minutes. Discard paper and foil, cool bowl to room temperature. Turn out just before serving.

White Sauce: Melt butter in pan, stir in flour, stir over heat until bubbling. Remove from heat, gradually stir in milk, stir over heat until sauce boils and thickens. Remove from heat, stir in cheese.

Lamb Sauce: Heat oil in pan, add onion and garlic, cook, stirring, until onion is soft. Add lamb, cook, stirring, until well browned. Stir in undrained crushed tomatoes, paste and basil. Bring to boil, simmer, uncovered, for about 10 minutes or until thickened.

Serves 6.

■ Recipe can be made 2 days ahead.
■ Storage: Covered, in refrigerator.
■ Freeze: Not suitable.
■ Microwave: Pasta and white sauce suitable.

RIGHT: From back: Creamy Lamb and Chicken Pasta Coil, Honeyed Lamb with Noodles and Omelette.

LAMB, CHEESE AND EGGPLANT TORTE

2 medium (about 600g)
    eggplants, sliced
salt
1/3 cup olive oil
1 tablespoon olive oil, extra
500g minced lamb
1 teaspoon ground cinnamon
1 teaspoon ground cumin
2 tablespoons tomato paste
425g can tomatoes
2 small chicken stock cubes,
    crumbled
1/2 teaspoon sugar
2 cups (200g) pasta twists
200g fresh goats' milk cheese,
    crumbled
1 1/2 cups (150g) grated mozzarella
    cheese
1 green pepper, chopped
1 tablespoon chopped fresh mint

Line base and side of deep 23cm round cake pan with paper, grease paper. Place eggplant slices on wire rack, sprinkle with salt, stand 20 minutes. Rinse eggplant slices under cold water, drain on absorbent paper.

Heat oil in pan, add eggplant in batches, cook on both sides until well browned; drain on absorbent paper.

Heat extra oil in pan, add lamb, cook, stirring, until well browned. Add spices, paste, undrained crushed tomatoes, stock cubes and sugar. Bring to boil, simmer, uncovered, for about 10 minutes or until thickened.

Add pasta to large pan of boiling water, boil, uncovered, until just tender; drain.

Combine pasta with lamb mixture in bowl. Combine cheeses, pepper and mint in separate bowl.

Place a layer of eggplant into prepared pan, spread with half the lamb mixture, top with half the cheese mixture. Repeat layering, finishing with an eggplant layer; press firmly into pan. Cover pan with foil, place pan in baking dish, pour in enough boiling water to come halfway up side of pan. Bake in moderate oven for 1 hour. Stand pan 10 minutes before turning out. Serve torte hot or cold, sprinkled with extra goats' milk cheese, if desired.
    Serves 8.

■ Recipe can be made a day ahead.
■ Storage: Covered, in refrigerator.
■ Freeze: Not suitable.
■ Microwave: Pasta suitable.

CHILLI GARLIC LAMB AND NOODLE STIR-FRY

500g lamb fillets, sliced
2 tablespoons chilli sauce
2 tablespoons hoi sin sauce
2 tablespoons sweet sherry
2 cloves garlic, sliced
500g packet fresh egg noodles
2 tablespoons oil
1 tablespoon oil, extra
1 bunch Chinese broccoli, chopped
1 teaspoon cornflour
1/2 cup water
2 tablespoons light soy sauce
2 teaspoons peanut butter

Combine lamb, chilli sauce, hoi sin sauce, sherry and garlic in bowl; cover, refrigerate 1 hour. Place noodles in bowl, cover with boiling water, stand 5 minutes; drain.

Heat half the oil in wok or pan, add half the lamb mixture, stir-fry until browned all over, remove from wok. Repeat with remaining oil and lamb.

Heat extra oil in wok, add broccoli, stir-fry until lightly cooked. Stir in blended cornflour and water, soy sauce and peanut butter, stir until mixture boils and thickens. Add lamb and noodles, stir until heated through.
    Serves 6.

■ Lamb can be prepared a day ahead.
■ Storage: Covered, in refrigerator.
■ Freeze: Not suitable.
■ Microwave: Not suitable.

ROAST LAMB WITH TOMATO ROSEMARY SAUCE

2kg leg of lamb
3 cloves garlic, sliced
6 small sprigs fresh rosemary
2 tablespoons olive oil
2 onions, sliced
2 x 410g cans tomatoes
2 tablespoons cornflour
2 tablespoons water
500g tagliatelle pasta
1 cup (80g) grated fresh
    parmesan cheese

Score lamb at 2cm intervals using sharp knife. Push garlic and rosemary into scores, brush lamb with oil. Place lamb in baking dish, bake in hot oven for 15 minutes, add onions and undrained crushed tomatoes to dish. Cover dish with foil, bake in moderate oven for about 1 hour or until done as desired. Remove lamb from sauce, cover, keep warm.

Combine sauce with blended cornflour and water in pan, stir over heat until sauce boils and thickens.

Add pasta to large pan of boiling water, boil, uncovered, until just tender; drain. Combine pasta with sauce, serve with sliced lamb; sprinkle with cheese.
    Serves 8.

■ Recipe best made just before serving.
■ Freeze: Not suitable.
■ Microwave: Pasta suitable.

RIGHT: Lamb, Cheese and Eggplant Torte.
FAR RIGHT: From back: Chilli Garlic Lamb and Noodle Stir-Fry, Roast Lamb with Tomato Rosemary Sauce.

CREAMY ASPARAGUS FETTUCINE WITH LAMB

1 tablespoon olive oil
500g lamb fillets, sliced
2 bunches (about 500g) fresh
**   asparagus**
40g butter
2 green shallots, chopped
1 small sprig fresh rosemary
300ml carton cream
½ cup grated fresh parmesan cheese
375g fettucine pasta

Heat oil in pan, add lamb, cook over high heat until browned all over. Remove from pan, drain on absorbent paper; keep warm.

Cut tips from asparagus, reserve tips. Cut stalks into 2cm lengths. Melt butter in pan, add stalks and shallots, cook, stirring, until asparagus is tender. Add rosemary and cream to pan, bring to boil, simmer, uncovered, for 10 minutes. Remove from heat, discard rosemary. Blend or process asparagus mixture until smooth, stir in cheese. Boil, steam or microwave reserved asparagus tips until tender; drain.

Add pasta to large pan of boiling water, boil, uncovered, until just tender; drain.

Combine pasta, lamb, asparagus sauce and asparagus tips in pan, cook until heated through.

Serves 6.

■ Recipe best made just before serving.
■ Freeze: Not suitable.
■ Microwave: Pasta and asparagus suitable.

LAMB RAVIOLI WITH MINTED YOGURT

2 tablespoons olive oil
1 small onion, finely chopped
1 clove garlic, crushed
200g minced lamb
1 teaspoon curry powder
1 teaspoon ground cumin
1 teaspoon cornflour
¼ cup water
2 quantities plain pasta dough

MINTED YOGURT
500g carton plain yogurt
1 tablespoon chopped fresh mint
1 tablespoon chopped fresh basil

Heat oil in pan, add onion and garlic, cook, stirring, until onion is soft. Add lamb, curry powder and cumin, cook, stirring, until lamb is browned. Stir in blended cornflour and water, bring to boil; cool.

Roll pasta dough until 1½mm thick, cut into 4½cm rounds, top half the rounds with ½ level teaspoon of lamb mixture. Brush edges of rounds with water, top with remaining rounds, press edges together. **Just before serving,** add ravioli to large pan of boiling water, boil, uncovered, for about 8 minutes or until just tender; drain. Combine ravioli with minted yogurt.

Minted Yogurt: Combine all ingredients in bowl; mix well.

Serves 4.

■ Pasta and sauce can be prepared a day ahead.
■ Storage: Covered, in refrigerator.
■ Freeze: Cooked pasta suitable.
■ Microwave: Not suitable.

LAMB CANNELLONI WITH CREAMY HERB SAUCE

105g packet instant cannelloni pasta

FILLING
2 tablespoons olive oil
400g minced lamb
410g can tomatoes
1 tablespoon tomato paste
2 tablespoons dry red wine
1 tablespoon chopped fresh chives
¼ cup grated fresh parmesan cheese
¼ teaspoon sugar

CREAMY HERB SAUCE
300ml carton cream
¼ cup chopped fresh chives
¼ cup chopped fresh parsley
1 tablespoon chopped fresh marjoram
½ cup milk
½ teaspoon seeded mustard
1 tablespoon cornflour
2 tablespoons dry white wine

Fill pasta with filling, place in single layer in greased shallow ovenproof dish. Pour sauce over cannelloni, bake, covered, in moderate oven for about 30 minutes or until pasta is tender.

Filling: Heat oil in pan, add lamb, cook, stirring, until well browned. Stir in undrained crushed tomatoes, paste and wine. Bring to boil, simmer, uncovered, for about 5 minutes or until thickened. Stir in chives, cheese and sugar; cool.

Creamy Herb Sauce: Heat cream in pan, add herbs, milk and mustard, bring to boil. Stir in blended cornflour and wine, stir until sauce boils and thickens.

Serves 4.

■ Recipe can be made a day ahead.
■ Storage: Covered, in refrigerator.
■ Freeze: Suitable.
■ Microwave: Suitable.

ABOVE LEFT: Clockwise from back: Creamy Asparagus Fettucine with Lamb, Lamb Ravioli with Minted Yogurt, Lamb Cannelloni with Creamy Herb Sauce.

FRUITY LAMB NOISETTES WITH ORANGE SAUCE

1 tablespoon risoni pasta
2 green shallots, finely chopped
40g sliced ham, chopped
60g ricotta cheese
½ teaspoon grated orange rind
¼ teaspoon chopped dried rosemary
1 tablespoon finely chopped dried papaw
700g boned loin of lamb
⅓ quantity herbed pasta dough
plain flour
30g butter, melted

ORANGE SAUCE
2 tablespoons dry white wine
2 tablespoons white wine vinegar
1 teaspoon grated orange rind
250g butter, chopped
2 green shallots, chopped

Add risoni to pan of boiling water, boil, uncovered, until just tender, drain; cool.

Combine risoni, shallots, ham, cheese, rind, rosemary and papaw in bowl. Spread mixture over inside of lamb, roll up, secure with string. Bake in very hot oven for 20 minutes, reduce heat to moderate, bake further 40 minutes or until tender.

Roll herbed pasta until 2mm thick, cut into 1½cm strips; sprinkle with flour.

Just before serving, cut lamb into 1½cm pieces. Add herbed pasta to large pan of boiling water, boil, uncovered, until just tender; drain. Wrap a strip of pasta around each piece of lamb, secure with toothpicks, place on oven tray, brush pasta with butter. Bake noisettes in moderately hot oven for about 20 minutes or until pasta is crisp. Serve with orange sauce.

Orange Sauce: Combine wine, vinegar and rind in pan, bring to boil, simmer, uncovered, until reduced to 1 tablespoon. Gradually whisk in cold butter. Add the shallots, mix lightly.

Serves 4.

■ Lamb can be cooked a day ahead. Sauce best made just before serving.
■ Storage: Covered, in refrigerator.
■ Freeze: Lamb suitable.
■ Microwave: Pasta suitable.

BELOW: Fruity Lamb Noisettes with Orange Sauce.
Below: Plate from Country Floors

WHOLEMEAL PASTA
AND LAMB LASAGNE

½ quantity wholemeal pasta dough
1 tablespoon olive oil
1 onion, sliced
2 cloves garlic, crushed
4 (about 400g) zucchini, sliced
2 teaspoons grated lemon rind
1 tablespoon olive oil, extra
2 cloves garlic, crushed, extra
750g minced lamb
1 small beef stock cube, crumbled
¼ cup chopped fresh parsley
¼ cup chopped fresh basil
2 tablespoons lemon juice
300g jarlsberg cheese, sliced
100g jarlsberg cheese, grated, extra
½ cup cream

Lightly grease shallow 18cm x 25cm ovenproof dish. Roll pasta dough until 2mm thick, trim sheets to fit prepared dish. Add pasta to large pan of boiling water, boil, uncovered, until just tender; drain.

Heat oil in pan, add onion and garlic, cook, stirring, until onion is soft. Add zucchini and rind, cook, stirring, until zucchini is lightly browned; remove from pan.

Heat extra oil in pan, add extra garlic and lamb, cook, stirring, until lamb is well browned and any liquid has evaporated. Add stock cube, herbs and juice, cook 1 minute.

Place 1 layer of pasta into prepared dish, spread with one-third each of the meat mixture, zucchini mixture and sliced cheese. Repeat layering, finishing with

pasta layer. Top with grated extra cheese, pour cream evenly over surface. Bake, uncovered, in moderate oven for about 30 minutes or until well browned and heated through.

Serves 6.

■ Recipe can be made a day ahead.
■ Storage: Covered, in refrigerator.
■ Freeze: Suitable.
■ Microwave: Pasta suitable.

ABOVE: Clockwise from front: Lamb with Broccoli in Red Wine Sauce, Wholemeal Pasta and Lamb Lasagne, Meatballs in Herbed Tomato Sauce.
RIGHT: Minted Green Pea Ravioli and Lamb Salad.

Right: Plate from Country Floors

LAMB WITH BROCCOLI IN RED WINE SAUCE

1/4 cup olive oil
1 onion, chopped
1 carrot, chopped
1 clove garlic, crushed
1/2 cup sweet sherry
1 cup dry red wine
1 1/4 litres (5 cups) water
2 large beef stock cubes, crumbled
1 bay leaf
1 tablespoon sugar
500g broccoli, chopped
1 red pepper, chopped
1/4 cup cornflour
1/4 cup water, extra
1 tablespoon cream
300g spaghetti pasta
1/4 cup olive oil, extra
600g lamb fillets, thinly sliced

Heat oil in pan, add onion and carrot, cook, stirring, until well browned. Add garlic, sherry, wine, water, stock cubes, bay leaf and sugar. Bring to boil, simmer, covered, for 20 minutes. Strain mixture, discard vegetables.

Return liquid to pan, bring to boil, boil, uncovered, for about 10 minutes, or until reduced by one-third. Add broccoli and pepper, boil until vegetables are tender. Stir in blended cornflour and extra water, stir until sauce boils and thickens, stir in cream; keep warm.

Add pasta to large pan of boiling water, boil, uncovered, until just tender, drain.

Heat extra oil in pan, add lamb, cook until well browned and tender. Combine lamb with sauce, serve with warm pasta.

Serves 4.

■ Sauce can be made a day ahead.
■ Storage: Covered, in refrigerator.
■ Freeze: Not suitable.
■ Microwave: Pasta suitable.

MINTED GREEN PEA RAVIOLI AND LAMB SALAD

600g lamb fillets
1 teaspoon cracked black
   peppercorns
1 clove garlic, crushed
1 tablespoon olive oil
1 quantity plain pasta dough

GREEN PEA FILLING
1 1/2 cups (180g) fresh or frozen peas
40g butter
1 onion, chopped
1 tablespoon chopped fresh mint

MINT DRESSING
1/4 cup olive oil
2 tablespoons cider vinegar
1/2 teaspoon sugar
1 1/2 tablespoons shredded fresh
   mint leaves

Combine lamb, pepper and garlic in bowl; cover, refrigerate 1 hour. Heat oil in pan, add lamb mixture, cook for about 5

minutes until well browned all over and tender, drain on absorbent paper; cool.

Cut lamb into thin slices. Roll pasta dough until 2mm thick, cut into 4cm rounds. Top half the rounds with 1/2 level teaspoons of pea filling, brush edges of rounds with water, top with remaining rounds, press edges to seal.

Add ravioli to large pan of boiling water, boil, uncovered, for about 5 minutes or until just tender; drain. Rinse ravioli under cold water, drain; cool. Combine ravioli, lamb and mint dressing in bowl.

Green Pea Filling: Boil, steam or microwave peas until soft, drain. Heat butter in pan, add onion, cook, stirring, until soft. Blend or process peas, onion mixture and mint until combined, but not smooth.

Mint Dressing: Combine all ingredients in jar; shake well.

Serves 6.

■ Ravioli can be prepared a day ahead. Salad can be made 2 hours ahead.
■ Storage: Covered, in refrigerator.
■ Freeze: Uncooked ravioli suitable.
■ Microwave: Filling suitable.

MEATBALLS IN HERBED TOMATO SAUCE

750g minced lamb
1 onion, chopped
2 cloves garlic, crushed
1 small beef stock cube, crumbled
1 1/2 cups (100g) stale breadcrumbs
1 egg, lightly beaten
plain flour
2 tablespoons olive oil
500g spaghetti pasta
2 tablespoons grated
   parmesan cheese

SAUCE
1 tablespoon olive oil
1 onion, chopped
1 clove garlic, crushed
410g can tomatoes
2 tablespoons tomato paste
1 1/2 tablespoons chopped fresh basil
1 tablespoon chopped fresh oregano
1 small beef stock cube, crumbled
1 cup water
1 teaspoon sugar

Combine mince, onion, garlic, stock cube, breadcrumbs and egg in bowl. Roll 1 level tablespoon of mixture into a ball, repeat with remaining mixture; cover, refrigerate 30 minutes.

Toss meatballs in flour, shake away excess flour. Heat oil in pan, add meatballs, cook until well browned all over; drain on absorbent paper.

Add pasta to large pan of boiling water, boil, uncovered, until just tender, drain; keep warm.

Just before serving, add meatballs to sauce, cover, simmer for about 10 minutes or until meatballs are tender. Sprinkle meatball sauce with cheese; serve with spaghetti.

Sauce: Heat oil in pan, add onion and garlic, cook, stirring, until onion is soft. Stir in undrained crushed tomatoes, paste, herbs, stock cube, water and sugar; bring to boil before adding meatballs.

Serves 6.

■ Meatballs can be made a day ahead.
■ Storage: Covered, in refrigerator.
■ Freeze: Meatballs suitable.
■ Microwave: Pasta suitable.

PORK & VEAL

Here you can enjoy tasty pork flavours such as salami, prosciutto, pancetta and cabanossi as well as familiar cuts of both pork and veal. There's a truly luscious pizza with a pasta base, a yummy pork and spinach roll, and little meatballs wrapped around melting, hot mozzarella – all quite hearty, as are the baked frittata and veal lasagne rolls. To tempt you even more, think of pretty salads and great-tasting sauces to make meals (or entrees) without fuss.

BUCATINI WITH PANCETTA AND TOMATOES

250g bucatini pasta
2 tablespoons olive oil
2 onions, finely chopped
250g pancetta, chopped
2 x 410g cans tomatoes,
   drained, chopped
4 (140g) bocconcini cheese, chopped

Add pasta to large pan of boiling water, boil, uncovered, until just tender; drain.

Heat oil in pan, add onions and pancetta, cook, stirring, until onions are soft. Stir in tomatoes, stir over heat for 2 minutes. Stir in bocconcini and pasta, stir until heated through.

   Serves 4.

■ Recipe best made just before serving.
■ Freeze: Not suitable.
■ Microwave: Pasta suitable.

PORK AND MACARONI SALAD

1⅓ cups (200g) macaroni pasta
½ cup peanut butter
½ cup water
2 teaspoons sesame oil
1½ tablespoons light soy sauce
1 tablespoon lime juice
pinch cayenne pepper
2 small green cucumbers, seeded
5 green shallots, chopped
300g barbecued red pork, sliced
lettuce leaves

Add pasta to large pan of boiling water, boil, uncovered, until just tender; drain. Rinse pasta under cold water; drain.

   Combine peanut butter, water, oil,

sauce, juice and cayenne in pan, stir over heat until smooth and combined.

   Cut cucumbers into strips, combine in bowl with shallots, pork and pasta. Pour over peanut butter mixture; mix well. Serve over lettuce leaves.

   Serves 4.

■ Recipe can be made 6 hours ahead.
■ Storage: Covered, in refrigerator.
■ Freeze: Not suitable.
■ Microwave: Suitable.

HERBED PROSCIUTTO, PEPPER AND PASTA BAKE

2 tablespoons olive oil
2 onions, chopped
1 leek, sliced
1 clove garlic, crushed
2 small fresh red chillies, chopped
1 large red pepper, chopped
1 large green pepper, chopped
⅓ cup chopped fresh basil
1 teaspoon dried oregano leaves
2 x 410g cans tomatoes
½ cup dry white wine
2 tablespoons tomato paste
2 small chicken stock cubes,
   crumbled
1 teaspoon sugar
¼ quantity spinach pasta dough
150g sliced prosciutto

Heat oil in pan, add onions, leek, garlic and chillies, cook, stirring, until onions and leek are soft. Add peppers, herbs, undrained crushed tomatoes, wine, paste, stock cubes and sugar. Bring to boil, simmer, uncovered, for 20 minutes.

   Cut pasta dough in half, roll each half

until 2mm thick. Cut pasta to fit shallow ovenproof dish (6 cup capacity).

   Add pasta to large pan of boiling water, boil, uncovered, for about 5 minutes or until just tender; drain. Spoon one-third of tomato mixture into dish, top with half the pasta. Place half the prosciutto over pasta. Repeat layering, ending with tomato mixture. Bake, covered, in moderate oven for about 40 minutes or until heated through.

   Serves 4.

■ Recipe can be made a day ahead.
■ Storage: Covered, in refrigerator.
■ Freeze: Not suitable.
■ Microwave: Pasta suitable.

RIGHT: Clockwise from front: Bucatini with Pancetta and Tomatoes, Pork and Macaroni Salad, Herbed Prosciutto, Pepper and Pasta Bake.

Dishes and rug from Mosmania

VEAL AND PASTA WITH MUSTARD CREAM SAUCE

¼ cup olive oil
1 onion, sliced
750g veal shank
plain flour
½ cup buttermilk
¾ cup cream
½ cup dry white wine
2 tablespoons French mustard
500g paglia e fieno pasta

Heat 1 tablespoon of the oil in pan, add onion, cook, stirring, until soft; remove from pan.

Remove meat from shank, cut meat into strips. Toss meat in flour, shake away excess flour. Heat remaining oil in pan, add meat, cook, stirring, until well browned and tender; remove from pan, combine with onion in bowl.

Boil any juices remaining in pan on high heat for about 1 minute or until reduced to about 1 tablespoon. Add buttermilk to pan, stir over heat until mixture thickens slightly. Stir in cream, wine and mustard, stir until mixture boils, simmer, uncovered, until slightly thickened.

Add pasta to large pan of boiling water, boil, uncovered, until just tender, drain; keep warm.

Add veal and onion to mustard sauce, stir until heated through, serve over pasta.
Serves 4.

■ Recipe best made close to serving.
■ Freeze: Not suitable.
■ Microwave: Pasta suitable.

QUICK TOMATO SAUCE WITH SALAMI AND BASIL

1 tablespoon olive oil
1 onion, thinly sliced
125g thinly sliced salami
410g can tomatoes
300g can Tomato Supreme
2 tablespoons chopped fresh basil
2 teaspoons sugar
250g penne pasta

Heat oil in pan, add onion and salami, cook, stirring, until onion is soft. Stir in undrained crushed tomatoes, Tomato Supreme, basil and sugar. Bring to boil, simmer, uncovered, for about 5 minutes or until sauce thickens.

Add pasta to large pan of boiling water, boil, uncovered, until just tender; drain. Combine pasta with sauce.
Serves 4.

■ Recipe best made just before serving.
■ Freeze: Not suitable.
■ Microwave: Pasta suitable.

LEFT: From back: Veal and Pasta with Mustard Cream Sauce, Quick Tomato Sauce with Salami and Basil.
RIGHT: Cheesy Pork and Spinach Roll.

Right: Plate from Country Floors

CHEESY PORK AND SPINACH ROLL

½ quantity plain pasta dough
¼ cup grated fresh parmesan cheese
3 teaspoons chopped fresh sage
60g butter, melted

FILLING
½ bunch (20 leaves) English spinach, shredded
1 tablespoon olive oil
1 small onion, finely chopped
1 clove garlic, crushed
200g pork and veal mince
150g cottage cheese
100g neufchatel cheese
1 egg, lightly beaten
½ teaspoon ground nutmeg

Cut pasta dough in half, roll each half to a 2mm thick square. Spread filling over each square, leaving 4cm border. Roll squares tightly as for a Swiss roll.

Wrap rolls in muslin, tie ends, place rolls in large pan filled with boiling salted water. Boil, uncovered, for about 20 minutes, turning rolls occasionally, or until rolls are firm to touch. Remove rolls from water; drain, remove muslin.

Cut rolls into 1½cm slices, arrange in single layer in greased flameproof dish, sprinkle with combined cheese and sage, drizzle with butter. Grill until pasta is lightly browned.

Filling: Boil, steam or microwave spinach until tender; drain, cool.

Heat oil in pan, add onion and garlic, cook, stirring, until onion is soft. Add mince, cook, stirring, until mince is well browned; cool slightly. Combine cheeses in bowl, stir in egg, nutmeg, mince mixture and spinach; mix well.

Serves 4.

■ Rolls can be made a day ahead.
■ Storage: Covered, in refrigerator.
■ Freeze: Not suitable.
■ Microwave: Spinach suitable.

DEEP-FRIED TORTELLINI WITH AVOCADO SAUCE

500g pork and veal tortellini
plain flour
2 eggs, lightly beaten
packaged breadcrumbs
oil for deep-frying

AVOCADO SAUCE
1 avocado, chopped
¼ cup milk
300ml carton thickened cream
1 tablespoon lemon juice
few drops tabasco sauce
1 tablespoon chopped fresh chives

Add tortellini to large pan of boiling water, boil, uncovered, until just tender; drain well on absorbent paper. Toss tortellini in flour, shake away excess flour. Dip tortellini in eggs, then breadcrumbs to coat; cover, refrigerate 1 hour.

Just before serving, deep-fry tortellini in hot oil until lightly browned; drain on absorbent paper. Serve hot tortellini with avocado sauce.

Avocado Sauce: Blend or process avocado and milk until smooth. Stir in cream, juice, tabasco and chives.

Serves 4.

■ Tortellini can be prepared a
  day ahead.
■ Storage: Covered, in refrigerator.
■ Freeze: Suitable.
■ Microwave: Not suitable.

SPICY PORK STIR-FRY WITH COCONUT MANGO SAUCE

800g pork fillets
¼ cup oil
1 onion, chopped
1 teaspoon tandoori curry paste
1 small fresh red chilli, chopped
150g can coconut milk
425g can mango slices, drained
2 teaspoons lime juice
⅔ cup water
1½ teaspoons paprika
3 zucchini, chopped
1 red pepper, chopped
150g snow peas
300g thin spaghetti pasta

Cut pork into 5cm strips. Heat oil in pan, add onion, cook, stirring, until soft. Add pork, curry paste and chilli, cook, stirring, until pork is well browned. Stir in coconut milk, mango, juice, water, paprika, zucchini and pepper. Bring to boil, simmer, covered, for 3 minutes; then simmer, uncovered, until sauce is slightly thickened. Add peas, simmer 1 minute.

Add pasta to large pan of boiling water, boil, uncovered, until just tender; drain. Serve pasta with pork and sauce.

Serves 6.

■ Recipe best made close to serving.
■ Freeze: Not suitable.
■ Microwave: Pasta suitable.

CHEESY LASAGNE PIZZA

240g packet lasagne pasta sheets
1 cup (125g) grated tasty cheese
250g mushrooms, sliced
1 small green pepper, chopped
2 x 125g cabanossi sticks, sliced
1½ cups (185g) grated tasty
  cheese, extra
¼ cup grated fresh parmesan cheese

TOMATO SAUCE
1 tablespoon olive oil
1 onion, chopped
2 cloves garlic, crushed
410g can tomatoes
2 tablespoons tomato paste
1 tablespoon Worcestershire sauce
2 tablespoons brown sugar
1 teaspoon dried basil leaves

Grease 25cm x 30cm Swiss roll pan. Add pasta to large pan of boiling water, boil, uncovered, until just tender; drain. Rinse pasta under cold water, drain.

Place half the pasta over base of prepared pan, sprinkle with tasty cheese, top with remaining pasta. Bake in moderate oven for 10 minutes.

Spread pasta base with tomato sauce, top with mushrooms, pepper and cabanossi. Sprinkle with extra tasty cheese and parmesan. Bake in moderately hot oven for about 40 minutes or until well browned.

Tomato Sauce: Heat oil in pan, add onion and garlic, cook, stirring, until onion is soft. Add undrained crushed tomatoes, paste, sauce, sugar and basil. Bring to boil, simmer, uncovered, for about 20 minutes or until sauce is thickened, stirring occasionally.

Serves 4.

■ Recipe can be made 2 days ahead.
■ Storage: Covered, in refrigerator.
■ Freeze: Cooked or uncooked
  pizza suitable.
■ Microwave: Pasta suitable.

RIGHT: Clockwise from left: Spicy Pork Stir-Fry with Coconut Mango Sauce, Deep-Fried Tortellini with Avocado Sauce, Cheesy Lasagne Pizza.

CREAMY MUSHROOM AND BACON PASTA SAUCE

250g fusilli pasta
1 tablespoon olive oil
1 onion, finely chopped
4 bacon rashers, thinly sliced
2 tablespoons pine nuts
250g mushrooms, thinly sliced
½ cup sour cream
1 egg, lightly beaten
¼ cup grated fresh parmesan cheese
¼ cup chopped fresh parsley

Add pasta to large pan of boiling water, boil, uncovered, until just tender, drain.

Heat oil in pan, add onion, bacon and pine nuts, cook, stirring, until onion is soft. Add mushrooms, cook, stirring, until mushrooms are soft. Stir in combined sour cream, egg, cheese and parsley, stir over low heat until heated through. Serve over pasta.

Serves 4.

■ Recipe best made just before serving.
■ Freeze: Not suitable.
■ Microwave: Pasta suitable.

VEAL LASAGNE ROLLS

500g veal steaks, chopped
2 tablespoons olive oil
1 onion, chopped
1 clove garlic, crushed
410g can tomatoes
1 cup water
2 tablespoons tomato paste
2 tablespoons chopped fresh parsley
240g packet instant lasagne
pasta sheets

WHITE WINE SAUCE
30g butter
2 tablespoons plain flour
1 cup milk
¼ cup dry white wine
½ cup grated tasty cheese
2 tablespoons chopped fresh parsley
1 tablespoon chopped drained capers
3 anchovy fillets, drained, chopped

Mince or process veal until fine. Heat oil in pan, add onion and garlic, cook, stirring, until onion is soft. Add veal, cook, stirring, until browned. Stir in undrained crushed tomatoes, water, paste and parsley. Bring to boil, simmer, uncovered, for about 30 minutes or until thickened. Allow mixture to cool for 5 minutes, blend or process until smooth.

Place pasta sheets into boiling water in batches, remove from heat, stand 5 minutes or until pliable; drain on absorbent paper.

Divide filling evenly over pasta sheets, roll up firmly. Place rolls in single layer in greased ovenproof dish, cover with sauce, bake, uncovered, in moderate oven for about 30 minutes or until rolls are tender.

White Wine Sauce: Melt butter in pan, add flour, stir over heat until bubbling.

Remove from heat, gradually stir in milk and wine. Stir over heat until sauce boils and thickens. Remove from heat, stir in cheese, parsley, capers and anchovies.

Serves 6.

■ Recipe can be made a day ahead.
■ Storage: Covered, in refrigerator.
■ Freeze: Uncooked rolls suitable.
■ Microwave: Not suitable.

BAKED PASTA FRITTATA WITH TOMATO WINE SAUCE

1½ cups (300g) risoni pasta
410g can tomatoes
250g mushrooms, chopped
200g salami, chopped
½ cup grated tasty cheese
4 eggs, lightly beaten
¼ cup chopped fresh parsley
½ cup packaged breadcrumbs
½ cup grated fresh parmesan cheese

TOMATO WINE SAUCE
½ cup water
¼ cup dry white wine
2 tablespoons tomato paste
2 tablespoons chopped fresh parsley

Lightly grease deep 23cm round cake pan. Add pasta to large pan of boiling water, boil, uncovered, until just tender; drain well.

Drain and chop tomatoes; reserve liquid for sauce. Combine tomatoes, mushrooms, salami, tasty cheese, eggs, parsley and pasta in bowl; mix well.

Combine breadcrumbs and parmesan cheese, add half to prepared pan, shake crumb mixture around base and side to coat evenly. Spoon pasta mixture into pan, press lightly, sprinkle with remaining crumb mixture.

Just before serving, bake in moderate oven for about 40 minutes or until well browned. Stand 5 minutes before turning out and cutting; serve with sauce.

Tomato Wine Sauce: Combine reserved tomato liquid with remaining ingredients in pan. Bring to boil, simmer, uncovered, for about 15 minutes or until thickened.

Serves 6.

■ Recipe can be prepared
  6 hours ahead.
■ Storage: Covered, in refrigerator.
■ Freeze: Not suitable.
■ Microwave: Pasta suitable.

LEFT: Clockwise from left: Veal Lasagne Rolls, Creamy Mushroom and Bacon Pasta Sauce, Baked Pasta Frittata with Tomato Wine Sauce.

Cloth from Les Olivades

VEAL AND CHEESE BALLS WITH BASIL CREAM SAUCE

⅔ quantity herbed pasta dough
500g veal steaks, chopped
½ cup grated fresh parmesan cheese
½ cup stale breadcrumbs
1 egg, lightly beaten
2 tablespoons chopped fresh basil
60g mozzarella cheese
plain flour
30g butter
1 tablespoon olive oil

BASIL CREAM SAUCE
30g butter
1 onion, chopped
¼ cup chopped fresh basil
½ cup cream
1 tablespoon cornflour
½ cup water

Roll pasta dough until 1½mm thick, cut into 2½cm x 30cm strips.

Mince or process veal, add parmesan cheese, breadcrumbs, egg and basil, process until combined. Cut mozzarella cheese into small cubes. Shape 1 level tablespoon of veal mixture around a mozzarella cube, roll into meatball; repeat with remaining veal mixture and mozzarella cubes. Toss meatballs lightly in flour, shake away excess flour.

Heat butter and oil in pan, add meatballs, cook until meatballs are well browned. Transfer meatballs to baking dish, bake, covered, in moderate oven for about 10 minutes or until cooked through.

Add pasta to large pan of boiling water, boil, uncovered, until just tender; drain. Serve meatballs with pasta and sauce.

Basil Cream Sauce: Melt butter in pan, add onion, cook, stirring, until soft. Add basil, cream, blended cornflour and water, stir until sauce boils and thickens.

Serves 4.

■ Meatballs and sauce can be made a day ahead.
■ Storage: Covered, in refrigerator.
■ Freeze: Meatballs suitable.
■ Microwave: Pasta and sauce suitable.

SPICY TORTELLINI SALAD

500g pork and veal tortellini
2 carrots
1 red pepper
1 green pepper
250g baby mushrooms, chopped
¼ cup black olives, sliced

PESTO DRESSING
¼ cup olive oil
¼ cup white vinegar
2 cloves garlic, crushed
¼ cup chopped fresh basil
2 tablespoons grated parmesan cheese
1 tablespoon tomato paste

Add tortellini to large pan of boiling water, boil, uncovered, until just tender; drain. Rinse tortellini under cold water; drain.

Cut carrots and peppers into thin strips. Combine tortellini, uncooked vegetables and olives in bowl, pour over dressing.
Pesto Dressing: Combine all ingredients in bowl; mix well.

Serves 4.

■ Salad can be made a day ahead.
■ Storage: Covered, in refrigerator.
■ Freeze: Not suitable.
■ Microwave: Not suitable.

CREAMY BACON AND BASIL TAGLIATELLE

500g tagliatelle pasta
1 tablespoon olive oil

SAUCE
4 bacon rashers, thinly sliced
300ml carton cream
⅓ cup dry white wine
2 teaspoons seeded mustard
2 tablespoons grated fresh parmesan cheese
1 tablespoon cornflour
2 tablespoons water
½ cup chopped fresh basil
6 green shallots, chopped

Add pasta to large pan of boiling water, boil, uncovered, until just tender; drain. Combine pasta and oil. Serve pasta topped with sauce.
Sauce: Cook bacon in pan until crisp. Stir in cream, wine, mustard, cheese and blended cornflour and water. Stir over heat until sauce boils and thickens. Stir in basil and shallots.

Serves 4.

■ Sauce can be made a day ahead.
■ Storage: Covered, in refrigerator.
■ Freeze: Not suitable.
■ Microwave: Pasta suitable.

LEFT: Veal and Cheese Balls with Basil Cream Sauce.
RIGHT: From back: Spicy Tortellini Salad, Creamy Bacon and Basil Tagliatelle.

Left: Tiles from Country Floors; napkin from Les Olivades. Right: Bowls from Amy's Tableware

HOT SPICY RAVIOLI WITH GARBANZO SALAD

1 quantity chilli pasta dough
plain flour
1 red pepper
1 green pepper
439g can garbanzos, rinsed, drained

FILLING
30g butter
1 onion, chopped
1 teaspoon white mustard seeds
1 clove garlic, crushed
150g chorizo sausage, chopped

DRESSING
⅓ cup olive oil ·
2 tablespoons lemon juice
½ teaspoon sugar
2 green shallots, chopped

Cut pasta dough in half, roll each half to a 2mm thick rectangle. Place ¼ level teaspoons of filling 3cm apart over 1 sheet of pasta. Lightly brush remaining pasta sheet with water, place over filling; press firmly between filling. Cut into square ravioli shapes; lightly sprinkle with flour.

Add ravioli to large pan of boiling water, boil, uncovered, for about 5 minutes or until just tender; drain. Rinse ravioli under cold water, drain; cool.

Quarter peppers, remove seeds and membrane, grill, skin side up, until skin blackens and blisters. Peel skin, cut peppers into thin strips.

Combine ravioli, peppers, garbanzos and dressing in bowl; mix well.
Filling: Melt butter in pan, add onion, mustard seeds and garlic, cook, stirring, until onion is soft. Blend or process onion mixture and sausage until finely chopped.
Dressing: Combine all ingredients in jar; shake well.

Serves 6.

■ Salad can be made 2 hours ahead.
■ Storage: Covered, in refrigerator.
■ Freeze: Uncooked ravioli suitable.
■ Microwave: Not suitable.

CANNELLONI SALAD WITH CUCUMBER YOGURT DRESSING

½ x 250g packet cannelloni pasta
2 hard-boiled eggs
1 cup (125g) grated tasty cheese
½ x 250g punnet cherry tomatoes, quartered
3 black olives, chopped
5 slices ham, chopped
2 green shallots, chopped
lettuce leaves

CUCUMBER YOGURT DRESSING
2 small green cucumbers, peeled, chopped
1 cup plain yogurt
1 tablespoon chopped fresh chives

Add pasta to large pan of boiling water, boil, uncovered, until just tender; drain. Rinse pasta under cold water; drain.

Push eggs through sieve, combine with cheese, tomatoes, olives, ham and shallots. Carefully spoon egg mixture into pasta. Serve pasta on lettuce leaves with dressing.
Cucumber Yogurt Dressing: Blend or process cucumbers until smooth, add yogurt, blend until combined; stir in chives.

Serves 6.

■ Salad can be made 6 hours ahead.
■ Storage: Covered, in refrigerator.
■ Freeze: Not suitable.
■ Microwave: Suitable.

PORK AND EGG SALAD WITH CHICKEN AND CHEESE

500g pasta crests
200g snow peas
1 cup (150g) chopped cooked chicken
4 hard-boiled eggs, halved
200g barbecued red pork, sliced
1 red pepper, chopped
1 stick celery, sliced
200g cheddar cheese, chopped
1 cos lettuce

DRESSING
¼ cup white vinegar
⅓ cup olive oil
2 tablespoons chopped fresh chives
1 teaspoon seeded mustard

Add pasta to large pan of boiling water, boil, uncovered, until just tender; drain. Rinse pasta under cold water; drain.

Boil, steam or microwave peas until just tender, rinse under cold water, drain. Combine peas, pasta, chicken, eggs, pork, pepper, celery and cheese in bowl; add dressing, toss lightly. Serve salad on lettuce leaves.
Dressing: Combine all ingredients in jar; shake well.

Serves 8.

■ Salad can be made a day ahead.
■ Storage: Covered, in refrigerator.
■ Freeze: Not suitable.
■ Microwave: Pasta and peas suitable.

PEPPERED CAPELLINI WITH PROSCIUTTO

150g capellini egg noodles
1 large lemon
1 orange
150g thinly sliced prosciutto
¼ cup olive oil
2 cloves garlic, crushed
4 green shallots, finely chopped
½ cup drained sun-dried tomatoes, sliced
⅓ cup finely grated fresh parmesan cheese
1 teaspoon cracked black peppercorns
1 tablespoon chopped fresh lemon thyme

Add noodles to large pan of boiling water, boil, uncovered, until just tender; drain. Rinse noodles under cold water; drain.

Using vegetable peeler, thinly peel rind from lemon and orange, avoiding white pith; cut rind into thin strips. Add strips to pan of boiling water, boil 1 minute; drain. Cut prosciutto into 1cm ribbons.

Heat oil in pan, add garlic and half the shallots, cook, stirring, until shallots are soft. Add prosciutto and rind, cook, stirring, until prosciutto is lightly browned; cool.

Combine pasta, prosciutto mixture, tomatoes, cheese, peppercorns and thyme in bowl; cover, refrigerate several hours. Sprinkle with remaining shallots before serving.

Serves 4.

■ Recipe can be made a day ahead.
■ Storage: Covered, in refrigerator.
■ Freeze: Not suitable.
■ Microwave: Pasta and rind suitable.

LEFT: Clockwise from back: Peppered Capellini with Prosciutto, Cannelloni Salad with Cucumber Yogurt Dressing, Hot Spicy Ravioli with Garbanzo Salad, Pork and Egg Salad with Chicken and Cheese.

Serving ware from Corso de Fiori

VEGETARIAN

You'll find inspiration here with the fresh, healthy appeal of vegetables adding to the pleasures of pasta in main courses and side dishes. For example, salads include an unusual fried tofu salad and a potato salad with a difference. Macaroni, so familiar, takes on new flair in our cheese sauce pie or nutty macaroni loaf. And among other favourites to sample are mushrooms, especially delicious in our double mushroom ravioli with burnt butter, and cheese and mushroom lasagne.

CHEESE TORTELLINI SALAD WITH MUSTARD MAYONNAISE

250g cheese tortellini
1 bunch (12 spears) fresh asparagus, chopped
200g green beans, chopped
1 small red pepper
1 small green pepper
100g baby mushrooms, chopped
4 green shallots, chopped

MUSTARD MAYONNAISE
2 egg yolks
1 tablespoon lemon juice
3/4 cup olive oil
1 tablespoon seeded mustard
1 clove garlic, crushed
2 teaspoons water

Add tortellini to pan of boiling water, boil, uncovered, until just tender, drain; cool.

Boil or steam asparagus and beans until just tender; drain, rinse under cold water. Cut peppers into thin strips. Combine tortellini, vegetables and shallots in bowl. Refrigerate several hours before serving with mustard mayonnaise.

Mustard Mayonnaise: Blend or process egg yolks and juice until pale and thick. With motor operating, gradually pour in oil in a thin stream; blend until thick. Stir in mustard, garlic and water.

Serves 4.

■ Salad can be made a day ahead.
■ Storage: Covered, in refrigerator.
■ Freeze: Not suitable.
■ Microwave: Vegetables suitable.

SPICY VEGETABLE STIR-FRY WITH PASTA

1/3 cup olive oil
1 onion, sliced
1 green pepper, chopped
1 medium eggplant, chopped
2 large tomatoes, peeled, chopped
1 stick celery, sliced
2 vegetable stock cubes, crumbled
1/2 teaspoon dried thyme leaves
2 bay leaves
1 tablespoon sambal oelek
1/2 cup water
1/2 cup dry red wine
200g snow peas, sliced
2/3 cup black olives
2 green shallots, chopped
375g penne pasta

Heat oil in pan, add onion and pepper, cook, stirring, until onion is soft. Stir in eggplant and tomatoes, cook over low heat for 5 minutes. Add celery, stock cubes, thyme, bay leaves, sambal oelek, water and wine. Bring to boil, simmer, uncovered, for 10 minutes. Stir in peas, olives and shallots; keep warm. Discard bay leaves.

Add pasta to large pan of boiling water, boil, uncovered, until just tender; drain.

Just before serving, toss pasta with vegetable mixture.

Serves 6.

■ Recipe best made just before serving.
■ Freeze: Not suitable.
■ Microwave: Pasta suitable.

TOMATOES AND BLACK BEAN PASTA SAUCE

500g fusilli pasta
1/4 cup olive oil
3 small fresh red chillies, chopped
3 cloves garlic, crushed
1/3 cup drained sliced sun-dried tomatoes
3 green shallots, sliced
2 tablespoons chopped fresh basil
1/2 teaspoon ground ginger
1/4 cup packaged salted black beans, chopped
410g can tomatoes
1/4 cup tomato paste
2/3 cup water
1/2 teaspoon Vecon
2 green shallots, chopped, extra

Add pasta to large pan of boiling water, boil, uncovered, until just tender, drain.

Heat oil in wok or pan, add chillies, garlic, sun-dried tomatoes, shallots, basil, ginger and beans, stir-fry for 1 minute. Add pasta, stir-fry until hot.

Blend or process undrained canned tomatoes until smooth, add to wok with paste, water and Vecon, stir-fry until hot. Serve sprinkled with extra shallots.

Serves 4.

■ Recipe best made close to serving.
■ Freeze: Not suitable.
■ Microwave: Pasta suitable.

RIGHT: Clockwise from front: Tomatoes and Black Bean Pasta Sauce, Cheese Tortellini Salad with Mustard Mayonnaise, Spicy Vegetable Stir-Fry with Pasta.

EGGPLANT, TOMATO AND FETA CHEESE SALAD

120g penne pasta
1 large (about 500g) eggplant,
    chopped
salt
¼ cup olive oil
1 onion, finely chopped
2 cloves garlic, crushed
2 x 410g cans tomatoes
⅓ cup tomato paste
2 teaspoons vinegar
3 teaspoons sugar
1 teaspoon dried oregano leaves
¼ cup black olives
200g feta cheese, chopped
4 green shallots, chopped

Add pasta to large pan of boiling water, boil, uncovered, until just tender; drain. Rinse pasta under cold water; drain.

Sprinkle eggplant with salt in bowl, stand for 30 minutes.

Rinse eggplant under cold water; drain well. Heat oil in pan, add eggplant, onion and garlic, cook, stirring, until onion is soft. Add undrained crushed tomatoes, paste, vinegar, sugar and oregano. Bring to boil, simmer, uncovered, until slightly thickened; cool. Stir in pasta, olives, cheese and shallots; mix well. Serve salad warm or cold.

Serves 4.

- Salad can be made a day ahead.
- Storage: Covered, in refrigerator.
- Freeze: Not suitable.
- Microwave: Pasta suitable.

POTATO AND PASTA SALAD WITH OLIVE VINAIGRETTE

750g potatoes
2 cups (400g) risoni pasta
2 tablespoons olive oil
2 teaspoons black mustard seeds
1 onion, chopped
1 clove garlic, crushed
¾ teaspoon ground cumin
1 small green pepper, thinly sliced
1 small red pepper, thinly sliced
1 tablespoon chopped fresh parsley

OLIVE VINAIGRETTE
½ cup pimiento-stuffed olives
⅓ cup orange juice
⅓ cup olive oil

Cut potatoes into 2cm cubes. Boil, steam or microwave potatoes until almost tender; drain, spread onto tray to cool.

Add pasta to large pan of boiling water, boil, uncovered, until just tender; drain. Rinse pasta under cold water; drain.

Heat oil in pan, add seeds, cook, stirring, until seeds begin to pop. Add onion and garlic, cook, stirring, until onion is soft; stir in cumin. Add potato, cook, stirring gently, until potato is lightly browned and tender; cool.

Combine potato mixture, pasta, peppers and parsley in bowl. Pour olive vinaigrette over potato mixture; mix gently.

Olive Vinaigrette: Blend or process all ingredients until smooth.

Serves 6.

- Salad can be made a day ahead.
- Storage: Covered, in refrigerator.
- Freeze: Not suitable.
- Microwave: Potatoes and pasta suitable.

PEPPERED PASTA AND CHEESE SALAD

2 cups (150g) shell pasta
2 red peppers
250g goats' milk cheese, chopped
¼ cup pine nuts, toasted
1 tablespoon small fresh
    marjoram leaves

DRESSING
2 tablespoons white vinegar
¼ cup olive oil
½ teaspoon cracked black
    peppercorns

Add pasta to large pan of boiling water, boil, uncovered, until just tender; drain. Rinse pasta under cold water; drain.

Quarter peppers, remove seeds and membrane. Grill peppers, skin side up, until skin blisters and blackens; cool slightly. Remove skin, cut peppers into long thin strips.

Combine peppers, pasta, cheese, nuts and marjoram in bowl, pour over dressing; toss well. Serve salad warm or cold.

Dressing: Combine all ingredients in jar; shake well.

Serves 6.

- Salad can be made a day ahead.
- Storage: Covered, in refrigerator.
- Freeze: Not Suitable.
- Microwave: Pasta suitable.

RIGHT: Clockwise from front: Peppered Pasta and Cheese Salad, Potato and Pasta Salad with Olive Vinaigrette, Eggplant, Tomato and Feta Cheese Salad.

CREAMY LEMON ZUCCHINI PASTA SAUCE

375g farfalle pasta
60g butter
1 clove garlic, crushed
2 small (about 180g) yellow zucchini
   or squash, sliced
150g green beans, halved
   lengthways
3/4 cup frozen peas, thawed
2 x 300ml cartons cream
1/4 cup lemon juice
1/2 cup (40g) grated fresh
   parmesan cheese
3 green shallots, sliced
2 tablespoons chopped fresh dill

Add pasta to large pan of boiling water, boil, uncovered, until just tender; drain.

Melt butter in same pan; cook garlic, zucchini and beans, stirring, until beans are just tender. Remove from pan. Add peas, cream, juice and cheese to pan; cook, stirring until heated through. Stir in pasta, vegetables, shallots and dill; cook, stirring, until sauce thickens slightly.

Serves 4

■ Recipe best made close to serving.
■ Freeze: Not suitable.
■ Microwave: Suitable.

FRESH HERB PASTA WITH HOT 'N' SPICY DRESSING

2 carrots
500g penne pasta
1/2 cup chopped fresh basil
1/2 cup chopped fresh mint
1/2 cup chopped fresh coriander
1/2 cup bean sprouts
2 teaspoons oil
2 cloves garlic, sliced
2 tablespoons unsalted
   chopped cashews

HOT 'N' SPICY DRESSING
2 tablespoons oil
1/4 cup olive oil
1 teaspoon sesame oil
1/4 cup lime juice
2 tablespoons light soy sauce
1/2 teaspoon sugar
2 teaspoons sambal oelek

Cut carrots into thin sticks. Add pasta to large pan of boiling water, boil, uncovered, until just tender; drain.

Combine pasta, carrots, herbs and sprouts in bowl; add dressing, toss well.

Heat oil in pan, add garlic, cook until lightly browned and crisp. Top salad with garlic and nuts.

Hot 'n' Spicy Dressing: Combine all ingredients in jar; shake well.
Serves 6.

■ Salad best made close to serving.
■ Freeze: Not suitable.
■ Microwave: Pasta suitable.

NOODLES AND VEGETABLES WITH SATAY DRESSING

150g fresh egg noodles
1 teaspoon sesame oil
425g can baby corn, drained
3 small green cucumbers, peeled
1 cup (100g) mung bean sprouts

SATAY DRESSING
2 tablespoons smooth peanut butter
2 tablespoons water
2 tablespoons light soy sauce
3 teaspoons sesame oil
2 tablespoons lime juice
2 teaspoons rice vinegar
2 cloves garlic, crushed
2 teaspoons grated fresh ginger
1 tablespoon sugar

Add noodles to pan of boiling water, boil, uncovered until just tender; drain. Toss noodles with oil in bowl.

Cut corn and cucumbers into strips, add to noodles with sprouts. Add dressing, toss well; serve warm or cold.
Satay Dressing: Combine all ingredients in pan, stir over heat until combined and heated through; do not boil.
Serves 6.

■ Recipe can be made a day ahead.
■ Storage: Covered, in refrigerator.
■ Freeze: Not suitable.
■ Microwave: Noodles suitable.

LEFT: Creamy Lemon Zucchini Pasta Sauce
RIGHT: From left: Fresh Herb Pasta with Hot 'n' Spicy Dressing, Noodles and Vegetables with Satay Dressing.

ONION RAVIOLI WITH THYME AND LEMON CREAM

2 tablespoons olive oil
3 red Spanish onions, sliced
2 hard-boiled eggs, chopped
½ teaspoon dried thyme leaves
1 quantity plain pasta dough

THYME AND LEMON CREAM
300ml carton cream
2 tablespoons chopped fresh thyme
½ teaspoon grated lemon rind
2 teaspoons cornflour
1 tablespoon water

Heat oil in pan, add onions, cook over low heat for about 10 minutes or until very soft; cool. Blend or process onions, eggs and thyme until almost smooth.

Cut pasta dough into quarters, roll each quarter until 2mm thick rectangle. Place ½ level teaspoons of filling 3cm apart over 2 of the pasta sheets. Brush remaining pasta sheets with water, place over filling, press firmly between filling and along edges of pasta. Cut into 3cm round ravioli shapes.

Just before serving, add ravioli to large pan of boiling water, boil, uncovered, for about 2 minutes or until tender; drain. Serve ravioli with thyme and lemon cream sprinkled with extra thyme, if desired.

Thyme and Lemon Cream: Combine cream, thyme and rind in pan, bring to boil, simmer, uncovered, for 5 minutes. Stir in blended cornflour and water, stir until sauce boils and thickens; strain.

Serves 4.

■ Ravioli can be prepared a day ahead.
■ Storage: Covered, in refrigerator.
■ Freeze: Uncooked ravioli suitable.
■ Microwave: Cream suitable.

THREE CHEESES AND MUSHROOM LASAGNE

1 tablespoon olive oil
1 onion, chopped
2 cloves garlic, crushed
1 red pepper, chopped
300g mushrooms, sliced
410g can tomatoes
1 tablespoon sugar
¼ cup tomato paste
1 cup water
½ teaspoon Vecon
250g packet cream cheese
250g cottage cheese
250g spinach lasagne pasta sheets
½ bunch (20 leaves) English spinach
2 cups (250g) grated tasty cheese

Lightly grease shallow ovenproof dish (8 cup capacity).

Heat oil in pan, add onion, garlic and pepper, cook, stirring, until onion is soft. Add mushrooms, undrained crushed tomatoes, sugar, paste, water and Vecon. Bring to boil, simmer, uncovered, for about 30 minutes or until thickened.

Beat cream and cottage cheese in bowl with electric mixer until smooth.

Add pasta to large pan of boiling water, boil, uncovered, until just tender; drain.

Spread small amount of tomato mixture over base of prepared dish, cover with single layer of pasta. Spread pasta with one-third of cheese mixture, cover with some of the spinach leaves, spread with one-third of tomato mixture. Repeat layering, ending with tomato mixture.

Bake, covered, in moderate oven for 1 hour, sprinkle with tasty cheese, bake, uncovered, for about 20 minutes or until lightly browned.

Serves 6.

■ Recipe can be made 2 days ahead.
■ Storage: Covered, in refrigerator.
■ Freeze: Suitable.
■ Microwave: Pasta suitable.

BAKED RED PEPPERS AND GARLIC WITH PASTA

4 large red peppers
2 cloves garlic, finely chopped
⅓ cup olive oil
1 tablespoon brown sugar
400g penne pasta
¼ cup shredded fresh basil

Cut peppers into strips, combine peppers, garlic, oil and sugar in a baking dish; mix well. Bake pepper mixture in moderate oven for about 1 hour or until peppers are soft.

Add pasta to large pan of boiling water, boil, uncovered, until just tender; drain. Return pasta to pan, stir in pepper mixture and basil.

Serves 4.

■ Recipe best made just before serving.
■ Freeze: Not suitable.
■ Microwave: Pasta suitable.

DEEP-DISH EGGPLANT AND PASTA TORTE

3 large (about 1.5kg) eggplants
salt
oil
375g penne rigate pasta
1 cup tomato-based pasta sauce
2 tablespoons tomato paste
1 cup (100g) grated mozzarella cheese
½ cup grated fresh parmesan cheese
1 tablespoon chopped fresh basil
2 eggs, lightly beaten
1 tablespoon packaged breadcrumbs

Grease deep 23cm round cake pan. Cut eggplants into 3mm slices, place slices on wire rack, sprinkle with salt, stand 20 minutes. Rinse eggplant under cold water; pat dry with absorbent paper.

Heat a little oil in pan, add eggplant slices in single layer, cook until lightly browned on both sides; drain. Repeat with more oil and remaining slices.

Add pasta to large pan of boiling water, boil, uncovered, until just tender; drain.

Combine pasta, sauce, paste, cheeses, basil and eggs in bowl. Centre a large eggplant slice in base of prepared pan, reserve about 10 slices for top. Place remaining eggplant slices around centre slice to cover base and side of pan.

Spoon pasta mixture into pan, arrange reserved eggplant slices over top, sprinkle with breadcrumbs.
Just before serving, bake in moderate oven for about 30 minutes or until firm. Stand 10 minutes before serving.
    Serves 6.

■ Recipe can be prepared a day ahead.
■ Storage: Covered, in refrigerator.
■ Freeze: Not suitable.
■ Microwave: Pasta suitable.

ABOVE: Clockwise from back left: Three Cheeses and Mushroom Lasagne, Baked Red Peppers and Garlic with Pasta, Onion Ravioli with Thyme and Lemon Cream, Deep-Dish Eggplant and Pasta Torte.

SPINACH TORTELLINI WITH TOMATO MUSHROOM SAUCE

250g packet frozen spinach, thawed
2 onions, finely chopped
1½ quantities tomato pasta dough
1 egg, lightly beaten

TOMATO MUSHROOM SAUCE
¼ cup olive oil
1 onion, chopped
2 cloves garlic, crushed
2 x 410g cans tomatoes
½ cup pine nuts
1 cup water
1 tablespoon sugar
150g mushrooms, chopped
2 tablespoons cornflour
2 tablespoons water, extra
½ cup chopped fresh parsley

Squeeze excess moisture from spinach, combine spinach with onions in bowl. Roll pasta dough until 2mm thick, cut into 5cm rounds. Brush rounds with egg, top each round with ½ level teaspoon of spinach mixture. Fold rounds in half, press edges together, pinch corners together.

Just before serving, add tortellini to large pan of boiling water, boil, uncovered, for about 5 minutes or until tender, drain; cool. Serve tortellini with tomato mushroom sauce.

Tomato Mushroom Sauce: Heat oil in pan, add onion and garlic, cook, stirring, until onion is soft. Add undrained crushed tomatoes, nuts, water and sugar. Bring to boil, simmer, uncovered, for 5 minutes. Add mushrooms, simmer, uncovered, further 10 minutes. Stir in blended cornflour and extra water, stir until sauce boils and thickens. Stir in parsley; cool.

    Serves 4.

■ Tortellini and sauce can be made a day ahead.
■ Storage: Covered, in refrigerator.
■ Freeze: Cooked tortellini and sauce suitable.
■ Microwave: Not suitable.

NUTTY MACARONI LOAF WITH YOGURT SAUCE

1 cup (125g) small macaroni pasta
1 cup (70g) stale breadcrumbs
1 cup (130g) ground cashews
1 cup (130g) ground brazil nuts
1 cup (80g) grated fresh
    parmesan cheese
1 cup (125g) grated tasty cheese
2 tablespoons sultanas
½ teaspoon garam masala
½ teaspoon turmeric
¼ teaspoon ground cumin
1 red pepper, finely chopped
2 tablespoons chopped
    fresh coriander
5 eggs, lightly beaten

YOGURT SAUCE
1 cup plain yogurt
2 teaspoons chopped fresh coriander
½ teaspoon garam masala

Grease 14cm x 21cm loaf pan, line base and sides with paper, grease paper. Add pasta to pan of boiling water, boil, uncovered, until just tender, drain; cool.

    Combine pasta, breadcrumbs, nuts, cheeses, sultanas, spices, pepper, coriander and eggs in bowl; mix well. Spoon mixture into prepared pan, smooth surface. Bake, uncovered, in moderate oven for about 30 minutes or until firm. Serve loaf hot or cold with sauce.
Yogurt Sauce: Combine all ingredients in bowl, mix well.

    Serves 6.

■ Recipe can be made 2 days ahead.
■ Storage: Covered, in refrigerator.
■ Freeze: Cooked loaf suitable.
■ Microwave: Pasta suitable.

DOUBLE MUSHROOM RAVIOLI WITH BURNT BUTTER

⅔ quantity tomato pasta dough
1 egg white, lightly beaten

FILLING
20g butter
1 onion, chopped
2 cloves garlic, crushed
200g mushrooms, chopped
200g shitake mushrooms, chopped
1 tablespoon chopped fresh tarragon

BURNT BUTTER
250g butter
1 tablespoon white vinegar

Cut pasta dough in half, roll each half until 2mm thick rectangle. Place level teaspoons of filling 3cm apart over 1 sheet of pasta. Lightly brush remaining sheet with egg white, place over filling, press firmly between filling and along edges of pasta. Cut into square ravioli shapes; lightly sprinkle ravioli with flour.
Just before serving, add ravioli to large pan of boiling water, boil, uncovered, for about 5 minutes or until just tender; drain. Serve ravioli with burnt butter.
Filling: Heat butter in pan, add onion and garlic, cook, stirring, until onion is soft. Add both mushrooms and tarragon, cook, stirring, until mushrooms are just tender.
Burnt Butter: Heat butter in pan until lightly browned, stir in vinegar.

    Serves 6.

■ Ravioli can be prepared a day ahead. Burnt butter best made just before serving.
■ Storage: Covered, in refrigerator.
■ Freeze: Not suitable.
■ Microwave: Burnt butter suitable.

LEFT: From front: Nutty Macaroni Loaf with Yogurt Sauce, Spinach Tortellini with Tomato Mushroom Sauce.
RIGHT: Double Mushroom Ravioli with Burnt Butter.

NO-COOK TOMATO ONION SAUCE WITH FRESH HERBS

1 red Spanish onion,
  finely chopped
2 large tomatoes, peeled, seeded,
  chopped
1 clove garlic, crushed
1 tablespoon lemon juice
¼ cup olive oil
1 teaspoon chopped fresh
  lemon thyme
½ teaspoon cracked black
  peppercorns
300g fusilli pasta
1 tablespoon shredded
  fresh basil

Cover onion with water in bowl, stand for 1 hour; drain. Combine tomatoes with onion, garlic, juice, oil, thyme and peppercorns in bowl; cover, refrigerate 1 hour.
Just before serving, add pasta to large pan of boiling water, boil, uncovered, until just tender; drain. Serve cold sauce over hot pasta, sprinkle with basil.
  Serves 4.

■ Sauce can be made a day ahead.
■ Storage: Covered, in refrigerator.
■ Freeze: Not suitable.
■ Microwave: Pasta suitable.

MACARONI AND SUN-DRIED TOMATO SALAD WITH PESTO

2 cups (250g) macaroni pasta
150g snow peas
150g baby mushrooms, halved
1 red pepper, finely chopped
½ cup drained sun-dried
  tomatoes, sliced

PESTO
1 bunch fresh basil
4 cloves garlic, crushed
2 tablespoons lemon juice
¾ cup olive oil
1 cup (100g) grated pecorino cheese

Add pasta to large pan of boiling water, boil, uncovered, until just tender; drain. Rinse pasta under cold water; drain.
  Boil, steam or microwave snow peas and mushrooms until just tender, rinse under cold water; drain. Combine pasta, vegetables, tomatoes and pesto in bowl, mix well; cover, refrigerate 1 hour before serving. Serve with lettuce, if desired.
Pesto: Blend or process basil leaves, garlic and juice until combined, gradually add oil in thin stream while motor is operating. Add cheese, process until combined.
  Serves 6.

■ Salad can be made a day ahead.
■ Storage: Covered, in refrigerator.
■ Freeze: Not suitable.
■ Microwave: Suitable.

LEFT: No-Cook Tomato Onion Sauce with Fresh Herbs.
ABOVE: Macaroni and Sun-Dried Tomato Salad with Pesto.

FRIED TOFU SALAD WITH CREAMY VEGETABLES

¾ cup farfalline pasta
2 carrots, grated
2 small zucchini, grated
2 sticks celery, chopped
1 red pepper, chopped
1 large tomato, chopped
¼ cup olive oil
150g firm tofu, cubed
1½ teaspoons cumin seeds
2 teaspoons white mustard seeds
¼ cup olive oil, extra
1 small fresh red chilli, chopped
1 medium (about 300g) eggplant, cubed
1 cup plain yogurt

Add pasta to large pan of boiling water, boil, uncovered, until just tender; drain. Rinse pasta under cold water; drain.

Combine pasta, carrots, zucchini, celery, pepper and tomato in bowl. Heat oil in pan, add tofu, cook, stirring gently, until browned, drain on absorbent paper. Add tofu to vegetable mixture.

Heat a dry pan, add seeds, cook, stirring, until seeds pop. Add extra oil, chilli and eggplant, cook, stirring, until eggplant is tender. Remove from heat, stir into vegetable mixture. Add yogurt; mix well. Serve salad on lettuce, if desired.

Serves 6.

■ Recipe can be made a day ahead.
■ Storage: Covered, in refrigerator.
■ Freeze: Not suitable.
■ Microwave: Pasta suitable.

MACARONI CHEESE SAUCE PIE

2 cups (200g) pasta elbows
1 tablespoon olive oil
1 small onion, chopped
1 clove garlic, crushed
1 small red pepper, sliced
½ cup canned drained corn kernels
2 zucchini, sliced
1 sheet ready rolled puff pastry
1 egg yolk

CHEESE SAUCE
40g butter
2 tablespoons plain flour
1½ cups milk
1 cup (80g) grated fresh parmesan cheese
1 cup (125g) grated tasty cheese
2 tablespoons chopped fresh parsley

Lightly grease deep ovenproof dish (8 cup capacity).

Add pasta to large pan of boiling water, boil, uncovered, until just tender; drain. Rinse pasta under hot water; drain.

Heat oil in pan, add onion, garlic and pepper, cook, stirring, until onion is soft. Combine onion mixture, pasta, corn, zucchini and cheese sauce in bowl; mix well. Spoon mixture into prepared dish.

Brush pastry with egg yolk, cut into 1cm strips. Place strips over filling in lattice pat-
tern, press gently against edge of dish; trim edges. Bake pie in moderately hot oven for about 15 minutes or until pastry is well browned.

Cheese Sauce: Melt butter in pan, stir in flour, stir over heat until bubbling. Remove from heat, gradually stir in milk, stir over heat until sauce boils and thickens slightly. Stir in cheeses and parsley.

Serves 6.

■ Pie can be made a day ahead.
■ Storage: Covered, in refrigerator.
■ Freeze: Cooked pie suitable.
■ Microwave: Pasta and sauce suitable.

PASTA WITH RED PEPPER AND CHILLI SAUCE

500g pipe rigate pasta
2 tablespoons grated parmesan cheese

RED PEPPER AND CHILLI SAUCE
2 red peppers
¼ cup drained chopped sun-dried tomatoes
1 small fresh red chilli, chopped
2 cloves garlic, crushed
1 teaspoon chopped fresh thyme
1 tablespoon tomato paste
¼ cup olive oil
½ teaspoon cracked black peppercorns

Add pasta to large pan of boiling water, boil, uncovered, until just tender, drain; keep warm. Add sauce to pasta, sprinkle with cheese.

Red Pepper and Chilli Sauce: Quarter peppers, remove membrane and seeds. Grill peppers, skin side up, until skin blisters and blackens; cool. Remove skin, chop peppers roughly.

Blend or process peppers with tomatoes, chilli, garlic, thyme, paste, oil and peppercorns until smooth.

Serves 4.

■ Sauce can be made a day ahead.
■ Storage: Covered, in refrigerator.
■ Freeze: Not suitable.
■ Microwave: Pasta suitable.

LEFT: Clockwise from front: Fried Tofu Salad with Creamy Vegetables, Pasta with Red Pepper and Chilli Sauce, Macaroni Cheese Sauce Pie.

DESSERTS

Although it sounds unusual to use pasta in sweet ways, you'll enjoy the interesting difference and appeal it adds to these very good desserts. Think of crisp cannelloni shells with creamy coconut ricotta filling, marzipan-filled ravioli with mocha sauce, and lasagne-based apple and almond custard flan. There are other luscious custards and creams, too, variously flavoured with caramel, fruit, nuts and spices. Quick ideas include apple butterscotch sauce and easy peanut honey sauce. We've even made chocolate pasta, and lavished it with raspberry sauce!

COCONUT CANNELLONI SNAPS WITH KIWI FRUIT SAUCE

18 cannelloni pasta
oil for deep-frying

KIWI FRUIT SAUCE
4 kiwi fruit, peeled
2 tablespoons icing sugar

FILLING
250g ricotta cheese
2 tablespoons coconut, toasted
1 tablespoon Malibu
¼ cup icing sugar

Add pasta to large pan of boiling water, boil, uncovered, until just tender; drain. Pat pasta dry with absorbent paper. Deep-fry pasta in batches in hot oil until lightly browned; drain on absorbent paper.
Just before serving, spoon filling into piping bag fitted with 5mm plain tube, pipe filling into cannelloni, serve cannelloni with sauce.
Kiwi Fruit Sauce: Blend or process kiwi fruit and sifted icing sugar until smooth; push through fine sieve.
Filling: Combine all ingredients in bowl; mix well.
  Serves 6.

- Recipe can be prepared a day ahead.
- Storage: Cannelloni shells, in airtight container. Filling and sauce, covered, in refrigerator.
- Freeze: Not suitable.
- Microwave: Pasta suitable.

SWEET PINK PASTA WITH WHITE CHOCOLATE SAUCE

1 cup plain flour
2 tablespoons icing sugar
1 egg, lightly beaten
red food colouring

WHITE CHOCOLATE SAUCE
½ cup milk
½ cup cream
250g white chocolate, grated
2 teaspoons Kahlua
pinch ground nutmeg

Combine sifted flour and icing sugar with egg and a tiny drop of colouring in food processor. Process until mixture forms a ball. Knead dough on lightly floured surface until smooth and evenly coloured; knead in more colouring, if desired.
  Roll dough through pasta machine on thickest setting, fold in half, repeat several times. Roll dough until 1mm thick using pasta machine. Cut into 1cm strips using fettucine attachment on machine.
  Add pasta to large pan of boiling water, boil, uncovered, for about 5 minutes or until just tender; drain. Serve warm pasta with warm sauce.

White Chocolate Sauce: Heat milk and cream in pan, do not boil. Remove from heat, add chocolate, stir until melted, stir in liqueur and nutmeg.
  Serves 4.

- Pasta and sauce can be made a day ahead.
- Storage: Covered, in refrigerator.
- Freeze: Not suitable.
- Microwave: Pasta suitable.

RIGHT: From back: Coconut Cannelloni Snaps with Kiwi Fruit Sauce, Sweet Pink Pasta with White Chocolate Sauce.

Plates from Accoutrement

EASY PEANUT HONEY SAUCE WITH RICE NOODLES

½ cup smooth peanut butter
½ cup warm water
¼ cup castor sugar
2 tablespoons honey
200g rice vermicelli noodles
oil for deep-frying

Blend or process peanut butter, water, sugar and honey until smooth.

Deep-fry noodles in batches in hot oil for about 10 seconds or until crisp; drain on absorbent paper. Serve sauce over noodles; top with mango slices, if desired.

Serves 4.

■ Sauce can be made several days ahead. Noodles best cooked just before serving.
■ Freeze: Not suitable.
■ Microwave: Not suitable.

APPLE AND ALMOND CUSTARD FLAN

2 cups milk
¼ cup custard powder
2 tablespoons castor sugar
½ cup milk, extra
410g can pie apples
⅓ cup sultanas
2 tablespoons brown sugar
2 tablespoons ground almonds
2 teaspoons plain flour
½ teaspoon ground cinnamon
¼ teaspoon ground nutmeg
pinch ground cloves
1 quantity plain pasta dough
2 tablespoons slivered almonds
icing sugar

Line base and side of 20cm springform tin with foil; grease foil. Bring milk to boil in pan, stir in blended custard powder, castor sugar and extra milk, stir until custard boils and thickens; cool.

Combine apples, sultanas, brown sugar, ground almonds, flour and spices in bowl.

Roll pasta until 2mm thick, cut into 3 rounds the same size as the prepared tin. Spread a little apple mixture over base of tin, spread with ¼ cup custard; top with a round of pasta.

Spread half the remaining apple mixture over pasta, then one-third of the remaining custard mixture. Repeat layering, finishing with a custard layer. Sprinkle custard with slivered almonds. Bake flan in moderate oven for about 30 minutes or until set; cool. Serve flan hot or cold, sprinkled with sifted icing sugar.

Serves 6 to 8.

■ Recipe can be made a day ahead.
■ Storage: Covered, in refrigerator.
■ Freeze: Not suitable.
■ Microwave: Not suitable.

DATE AND NUT TORTELLINI WITH CHERRY CUSTARD

⅓ cup chopped dates
3 teaspoons Creme de Cacao
40g white chocolate, melted
75g packaged cream cheese, softened
¼ teaspoon ground cinnamon
⅓ cup chopped roasted hazelnuts
½ quantity plain pasta dough
1 egg, lightly beaten

CHERRY CUSTARD
3 egg yolks
¼ cup castor sugar
300ml carton thickened cream
1 tablespoon Kirsch
425g can stoneless black cherries, drained

Combine dates and liqueur in bowl; cover, stand 1 hour.

Blend or process date mixture, chocolate, cheese and cinnamon until smooth; stir in nuts.

Cut pasta dough in half, roll each half until 1mm thick, cut into 8cm rounds. Top each round with 1 level teaspoon of date mixture, brush edges of rounds with water, fold in half, pressing edges to seal. Brush corners with water, pinch together. Lightly sprinkle tortellini with extra flour.

Add pasta to large pan of boiling water, boil, uncovered, until just tender; drain.

Just before serving, place tortellini on lightly greased oven tray, brush with egg, bake in hot oven for about 15 minutes or until lightly browned. Serve hot with cherry custard.

Cherry Custard: Beat egg yolks and sugar in small bowl with electric mixer until thick and pale. Heat cream in pan until bubbles appear, do not boil. Whisk egg yolk mixture into cream, stir over heat, without boiling, until mixture thickens slightly, stir in liqueur. Add cherries.

Serves 6 to 8.

■ Tortellini can be prepared a day ahead. Custard can be made a day ahead.
■ Storage: Covered, in refrigerator.
■ Freeze: Uncooked tortellini suitable.
■ Microwave: Not suitable.

LEFT: From front: Apple and Almond Custard Flan, Easy Peanut Honey Sauce with Rice Noodles.
BELOW: Date and Nut Tortellini with Cherry Custard.

Left: Plates and bouquet from Home & Garden

CARAMEL SULTANA CUSTARD WITH PEARS

⅔ cup conchigliette pasta
2 cups milk
⅓ cup sultanas
⅓ cup caramel topping
2 eggs, separated
4 canned drained pear halves, sliced

Combine pasta and milk in pan, bring to boil, simmer, uncovered, for 10 minutes, stirring occasionally. Transfer mixture to bowl; cool to room temperature.

Add sultanas, topping and egg yolks to pasta mixture; mix well.

Beat egg whites in small bowl with electric mixer until soft peaks form, gently fold into pasta mixture.

Divide mixture between 4 ovenproof dishes (¾ cup capacity), top with pears. Cover dishes, place dishes in baking dish, pour enough boiling water into baking dish to come halfway up sides of dishes. Bake in moderate oven for about 25 minutes or until firm.

Serves 4.

114

MARZIPAN RAVIOLI WITH MOCHA SAUCE

1 cup plain flour
¼ cup pure icing sugar
1 egg, lightly beaten
1 teaspoon water, approximately
30g milk chocolate, melted
2 tablespoons flaked almonds, toasted

FILLING
½ x 200g roll prepared marzipan, chopped
60g milk chocolate, grated
2 teaspoons water

MOCHA SAUCE
300ml carton thickened cream
2 teaspoons dry instant coffee
2 tablespoons castor sugar
1 teaspoon cornflour
½ cup milk
¼ cup Kahlua

Sift flour and icing sugar into bowl, gradually stir in egg and enough water to mix to a firm dough. Process mixture for 30 seconds or turn onto lightly floured surface and knead gently for about 3 minutes or until mixture is well combined, adding a little water if necessary (mixture should be dry, but not flaky).

Cut pasta dough in half, roll each half until 1mm thick rectangle. Place ¼ level teaspoons of filling 3cm apart over 1 sheet of pasta. Lightly brush remaining sheet with water, place over filling; press firmly between filling and along edges. Cut into square ravioli shapes between filling. Lightly sprinkle ravioli with a little extra flour.

Just before serving, add ravioli to large pan of boiling water, boil, uncovered, for about 5 minutes or until tender; drain. Serve warm ravioli with warm mocha sauce, drizzle with chocolate and sprinkle with almonds.

Filling: Beat all ingredients in small bowl with electric mixer until smooth.

Mocha Sauce: Combine cream, coffee and sugar in pan. Stir in blended cornflour and milk, stir over heat until sauce boils and thickens; stir in liqueur.

Serves 6.

■ Ravioli can be made 2 days ahead. Sauce can be made 3 hours ahead.
■ Storage: Covered, in refrigerator.
■ Freeze: Not suitable.
■ Microwave: Sauce suitable.

BAKED PEACH AND PECAN CRUMBLES

1½ cups (125g) fusilli pasta
3 peaches, peeled, sliced
1 teaspoon grated orange rind
⅓ cup orange juice
2 tablespoons water
1 stick cinnamon
2 tablespoons brown sugar
2 teaspoons arrowroot
2 teaspoons water, extra
½ cup stale breadcrumbs
¼ cup chopped glace ginger
¼ teaspoon mixed spice
½ cup chopped pecans
¼ cup brown sugar, extra
30g butter, melted

SPICED CREAM
1 cup thickened cream
2 teaspoons castor sugar
¼ teaspoon mixed spice

Add pasta to large pan of boiling water, boil, uncovered, until just tender; drain.

Combine peaches, rind, juice, water, cinnamon and sugar in pan, stir over heat until sugar is dissolved. Bring to boil, simmer, covered, for about 10 minutes or until peaches are soft; remove cinnamon stick. Stir in blended arrowroot and extra water, stir over heat until mixture boils and thickens; cool.

Grease 4 ovenproof dishes (1 cup capacity), sprinkle with breadcrumbs. Divide half the pasta between dishes; top with peach mixture and ginger. Divide remaining pasta between dishes, sprinkle with combined spice, nuts and extra sugar.

Just before serving, drizzle butter over crumbles, place dishes on oven tray, bake in moderate oven for about 25 minutes or until well browned. Serve warm with spiced cream.

Spiced Cream: Beat all ingredients in small bowl with electric mixer until soft peaks form.

Serves 4.

■ Crumbles can be prepared a day ahead. Spiced cream best prepared just before serving.
■ Storage: Covered, in refrigerator.
■ Freeze: Not suitable.
■ Microwave: Pasta suitable.

■ Recipe best made just before serving.
■ Freeze: Not suitable.
■ Microwave: Not suitable.

ABOVE LEFT: Clockwise from front: Marzipan Ravioli with Mocha Sauce, Caramel Sultana Custard with Pears, Baked Peach and Pecan Crumbles.

Coffee set from Bodum

CARAMEL CREAM CUSTARDS

½ **cup fusilli pasta**
¾ **cup castor sugar**
½ **cup water**

CUSTARD
6 eggs
1 teaspoon ground cinnamon
⅓ **cup castor sugar**
300ml carton thickened cream
1 cup milk

Add pasta to large pan of boiling water, boil, uncovered, until just tender; drain.

Combine sugar and water in pan, stir over heat until sugar is dissolved. Bring to boil, boil, uncovered, without stirring, for about 5 minutes or until golden brown.

Pour toffee over bases of 6 ovenproof moulds (¾ cup capacity). Toffee will set at this stage. Spoon pasta into moulds, pour custard over pasta.

Place moulds in baking dish, pour in enough boiling water to come halfway up sides of moulds. Bake, uncovered, in moderate oven for about 40 minutes or until custard is just set. Remove moulds from baking dish, cool to room temperature; cover, refrigerate overnight.

Just before serving, run a thin-bladed knife around edge of each mould, turn custards onto plates. Serve with blanched orange rind strips, if desired.

Custard: Whisk eggs, cinnamon and sugar together in bowl. Combine cream and milk in pan, bring to boil. Gradually whisk milk mixture into egg mixture.

Serves 6.

■ Custards can be made 3 days ahead.
■ Storage: Covered, in refrigerator.
■ Freeze: Not suitable.
■ Microwave: Pasta suitable.

MANGO ORANGE CREAMS WITH PASSIONFRUIT SYRUP

1 cup orange juice
3 cups water
18 extra large pasta shells
1 large mango, finely chopped
250g ricotta cheese
2 tablespoons castor sugar

PASSIONFRUIT SYRUP
⅓ **cup fresh passionfruit pulp**
½ **cup sugar**
1 cup water

116

CHOCOLATE PASTA TENDRILS WITH RASPBERRY SAUCE

1 cup plain flour
2 eggs, lightly beaten
60g dark chocolate, melted
2 tablespoons cocoa
1 tablespoon icing sugar

RASPBERRY SAUCE
3 cups (350g) fresh or frozen
   raspberries
⅓ cup castor sugar
⅓ cup water

Process flour, eggs, chocolate, cocoa and icing sugar until mixture forms a ball. Knead dough on lightly floured surface for 10 minutes. Roll dough until 1mm thick using pasta machine. Cut into 1mm strips using pasta machine.

Add pasta to large pan of boiling water, boil, uncovered, for about 3 minutes or until just tender; drain. Rinse pasta under cold water; drain. Serve pasta with raspberry sauce.

Raspberry Sauce: Combine all ingredients in pan, stir over heat until sugar is dissolved. Cook, uncovered, for about 3 minutes or until berries are soft. Push mixture through sieve to remove seeds; cover, refrigerate until cold.
   Serves 4.

■ Pasta and sauce can be made a day ahead.
■ Storage: Covered, in refrigerator.
■ Freeze: Sauce suitable.
■ Microwave: Pasta suitable.

LEFT: From left: Mango Orange Creams with Passionfruit Syrup, Caramel Cream Custards. BELOW: Chocolate Pasta Tendrils with Raspberry Sauce.

Left and below: China from Villeroy & Boch

Bring orange juice and water to boil in pan, add pasta, boil, uncovered, until pasta is just tender; drain; cool.

Combine mango, cheese and sugar in bowl; mix well. Fill pasta shells with mango mixture. Serve shells with passionfruit syrup.

Passionfruit Syrup: Combine all ingredients in pan, stir over heat until sugar is dissolved. Bring to boil, simmer, uncovered, for 5 minutes or until slightly thickened; cool.
   Serves 6.

■ Filling and syrup can be made a day ahead.
■ Storage: Covered, in refrigerator.
■ Freeze: Not suitable.
■ Microwave: Pasta suitable.

MERINGUE-TOPPED CITRUS RISONI PUDDING

2/3 cup risoni pasta
1½ cups milk
1 teaspoon grated lemon rind
1 teaspoon grated orange rind
¼ cup finely chopped glace apricots
½ cup sour cream
4 egg yolks
¼ cup cornflour
½ cup castor sugar
¼ cup lemon juice
¼ cup orange juice
1 cup milk, extra

MERINGUE TOPPING
4 egg whites
⅓ cup castor sugar
2 tablespoons slivered almonds, toasted
1 tablespoon currants

Combine pasta, milk and rinds in pan, stir until boiling. Simmer, covered, for about 10 minutes or until pasta is tender and mixture is thick; stir several times during cooking. Remove from heat, stir in apricots and sour cream; cool.

Beat egg yolks, cornflour and sugar to a paste in pan, stir in juices and extra milk, stir mixture over heat until custard boils and thickens. Stir custard into pasta mixture. Spread mixture over base of deep ovenproof dish (4 cup capacity).

Just before serving, spread custard mixture with topping. Bake in moderate oven for about 5 minutes or until topping is lightly browned.

Meringue Topping: Beat egg whites in small bowl with electric mixer until soft peaks form, gradually add sugar, beating until dissolved between each addition. Fold in almonds and currants.

Serves 6.

- Recipe can be prepared a day ahead.
- Storage: Covered, in refrigerator.
- Freeze: Not suitable.
- Microwave: Not suitable.

FETTUCINE WITH APPLE BUTTERSCOTCH SAUCE

3 cups apple juice
150g fettucine pasta

APPLE BUTTERSCOTCH SAUCE
2 large apples, peeled
1 tablespoon sugar
¼ cup water
¼ teaspoon ground cinnamon
50g butter
2/3 cup brown sugar, firmly packed
½ cup thickened cream
1 teaspoon rum

Bring juice to boil in pan, add pasta, boil, uncovered, until just tender; drain. Serve hot sauce over hot pasta.

Apple Butterscotch Sauce: Slice apples thinly, combine in pan with sugar, water and cinnamon, bring to boil, simmer, covered, for about 10 minutes or until tender; drain.

Melt butter in pan, add brown sugar and cream, stir until combined. Bring to boil, simmer, uncovered, without stirring, for 5 minutes. Remove from heat, stir in rum and apples.

Serves 4.

- Recipe can be made 3 hours ahead.
- Storage: Covered, at room temperature.
- Freeze: Not suitable.
- Microwave: Pasta suitable.

APRICOT NOODLE CREAM

250g fusilli bucati lunghi pasta
1 2/3 cups (250g) chopped dried apricots
4 eggs, lightly beaten
1 cup cream
½ cup milk
½ cup castor sugar
½ teaspoon ground nutmeg
½ teaspoon ground cinnamon
½ teaspoon castor sugar, extra

Add pasta to large pan of boiling water, boil, uncovered, until just tender, drain; cool. Soak apricots in boiling water for 5 minutes, drain; cool.

Combine eggs, cream, milk, sugar and half each of the nutmeg and cinnamon in bowl, stir in pasta and apricots. Pour mixture into a shallow ovenproof dish (4 cup capacity). Combine remaining nutmeg and cinnamon with extra sugar, sprinkle over pasta mixture.

Place dish in baking dish, pour enough boiling water into baking dish to come halfway up sides of dish. Bake in moderate oven for about 40 minutes or until just set.

Serves 4.

- Recipe best made just before serving.
- Freeze: Not suitable.
- Microwave: Pasta suitable.

RIGHT: Clockwise from front: Fettucine with Apple Butterscotch Sauce, Meringue-Topped Citrus Risoni Pudding, Apricot Noodle Cream.

China from Villeroy & Boch; cloth from Les Olivades

HOW TO MAKE FRESH PASTA

Step-by-Step Guide

With our easy instructions and pictures, you can soon learn to make fresh pasta by hand or machine; use quantities of plain or flavoured pasta dough as specified in individual recipes. We also give more details on how to cook pasta (including how to microwave it), and how to reheat it correctly.

Here are recipes for plain pasta dough and the flavour variations we used in this book:

PLAIN PASTA

2 cups plain flour
3 eggs

HAND METHOD

1. Sift flour onto bench or into bowl, make well in centre, add eggs to well. Using fingers, gradually mix flour into eggs.

2. Press mixture into a ball.

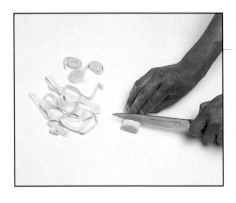

3. Knead dough for about 10 minutes or until smooth and elastic. Cover dough, stand 20 minutes.

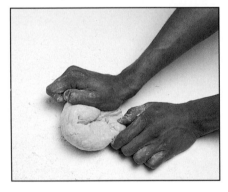

4. Roll dough on lightly floured surface to desired thickness.

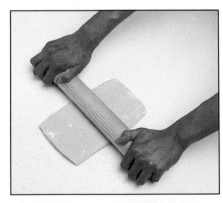

5. To make fettucine or tagliatelle pasta, roll sheets of pasta dough firmly. Cut roll into slices, unroll slices into strips.

MACHINE METHOD

1. Combine ingredients in food processor.

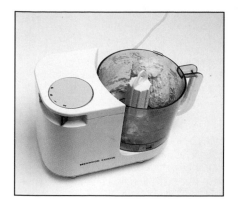

2. Process ingredients until mixture forms a ball.

3. Knead dough on lightly floured surface until smooth. Cut dough in half, roll each half through pasta machine set on thickest setting. Fold dough in half, roll through machine. Repeat folding and rolling several times until dough is very smooth and elastic, dusting dough with a little extra flour, when necessary.

4. Roll dough through machine, adjusting setting to become less thick with each roll, dusting dough with a little extra flour, when necessary. Roll to desired thickness.

5. To make fettucine, roll dough through fettucine attachment of machine, dusting dough with a little extra flour, when necessary.

WHOLEMEAL PASTA

1¼ cups plain flour
¾ cup wholemeal plain flour
3 eggs

Make as for plain pasta dough.

CHILLI PASTA

2 cups plain flour
1 teaspoon chilli powder
3 eggs

Make as for plain pasta dough, combining chilli powder with flour.

SPINACH PASTA

¼ cup chopped cooked spinach
2½ cups plain flour
2 eggs

Squeeze excess moisture from spinach, add to flour with eggs. Continue as for plain pasta dough.

PEPPER PASTA

2 cups plain flour
1½ teaspoons seasoned pepper
1 teaspoon paprika
3 eggs

Make as for plain pasta dough, combining pepper and paprika with flour.

HERBED PASTA

2 cups plain flour
¼ cup chopped fresh basil
3 eggs

Make as for plain pasta dough, adding basil with eggs.

TOMATO PASTA

1¾ cups plain flour
80g sachet tomato soup mix
3 eggs

Make as for plain pasta dough, combining soup mix with flour.

TO MAKE RAVIOLI

Roll pasta dough as specified in individual recipes, place filling at even intervals over dough. Brush lightly between filling and along edges with water. Top with a sheet of pasta, press firmly between filling and along edges. Cut into ravioli shapes using a pastry wheel; follow size indicated in individual recipes. Cook as specified in individual recipes.

TO MAKE TORTELLINI

Roll pasta dough to desired thickness, cut into rounds following size indicated in individual recipes. Top rounds with filling, lightly brush edges of rounds with water, fold rounds in half, press edges together to seal. Fold edges up, press corners together firmly. Cook as specified in individual recipes.

PASTA FACTS

Many nations claim to have invented macaroni (the generic term for all shapes and flavours of pasta) but it is in Italy that pasta-making was perfected. As a result, most of the macaronis bear Italian names. When these names are translated, they describe the shape or type of pasta: lasagne means "broad-leafed"; farfalle is "butterfly", and so on.

Macaroni products can be divided into four basic groups — cords, tubes, ribbons, and special shapes such as shells, crests, etc. There is a wide range of sizes and shapes within each group. Ravioli and tortellini are small shapes with fillings of cheese, vegetables, beef, pork, chicken, etc.

Pasta can be fresh or dried; one can be substituted for the other. Use the same weight as specified for dried or fresh when substituting.

The noodles we used are mostly of oriental origin; these are available in different types and sizes, including wonton wrappers. A big difference between pasta and noodles is the type of recipes they are used in. We used noodles mostly in recipes with an Asian influence, although occasionally we used wonton wrappers, etc., as a convenient pastry for ravioli.

TO COOK PASTA

Cook all forms of pasta in plenty of boiling water. Use a large saucepan or small boiler. Three-quarters fill the pan with hot water, cover, place over high heat, bring water to a fast rolling boil, add sprinkling of salt, if desired. Add pasta gradually, so water does not go off the boil.

When cooking spaghetti, vermicelli or any of the "long goods", as they are called, hold long strands at one end, place other ends in the boiling water. The pasta will begin to soften in the hot water and it is then simple to lower strands into saucepan, coiling them neatly inside pan.

Check individual recipes or instructions on packet for cooking times. Cooking time of pasta varies according to individual manufacturers; freshness of the product, too, will affect cooking time (home-made pasta cooks much more quickly than the commercial product). Pasta should not be overcooked; it should be "al dente" (to the tooth) – tender but firm.

TO MICROWAVE PASTA

You can microwave fresh and dried pasta successfully, though each takes about the same time as in conventional cooking.

Place pasta in large microwave proof bowl, pour in enough boiling water to cover pasta generously. Microwave, covered, on HIGH, until pasta is just tender; drain. Take care not to overcook pasta.

TO REHEAT PASTA

Place pasta in heatproof bowl, add enough boiling water to cover pasta, stand for I minute; drain well.

TO REHEAT PASTA IN A MICROWAVE OVEN

Place pasta in microwave proof bowl, cover, microwave on HIGH for 1 minute at a time, stirring occasionally, or until heated through; drain well.

Glossary

Here are some terms, names and
alternatives to help everyone use and understand our recipes perfectly.

ALCOHOL: is optional but gives special flavour. You can use fruit juice or water instead to make up the liquid content in our recipes.

ALMONDS:
Flaked: sliced almonds.
Ground: we used commercially ground packaged almonds.
Slivered: almonds cut into slivers.
ARROWROOT: used mostly for thickening. Cornflour can be used instead.
BACON RASHERS: bacon slices.
BALMAIN BUG: crustacean first discovered in Sydney Harbour, NSW; named after the harbourside suburb of Balmain. Crab or lobster can be substituted.

Balmain bugs.

BEAN SPROUTS: we used mung bean sprouts; these should be topped and tailed; available fresh or canned in brine.
BEANS, BLACK: are fermented, salted soya beans. Canned and dried black beans can be substituted. Drain and rinse canned variety, soak and rinse dried variety. Leftover beans will keep for months in an airtight container in the refrigerator. Mash beans when cooking to release flavour.

BEEF:
Chuck steak: is cut from the neck of the animal. Flesh is firm, with coarse grain, red colour and little fat. Long cooking is recommended.
Eye-fillet: tenderloin.
Minced: ground beef.
BREADCRUMBS:
Packaged: use fine packaged breadcrumbs.
Stale: use 1 or 2-day-old white bread made into crumbs by grating, blending or processing.

BROCCOLI, CHINESE (gai lum): remove and discard fibrous parts of the stem, cut flowerets away from stems and leaves. If using remaining stems, peel away any tough skin with peeler and chop stems.

Chinese broccoli.

BUTTER: use salted or unsalted (sweet) butter; 125g is equal to 1 stick butter.

BUTTERMILK: is now made by adding a culture to skim milk to give a slightly acid flavour; skim milk can be substituted if preferred.

CABANOSSI: a type of sausage; also known as cabana.

From top: Chorizo sausage, cabanossi.

CABBAGE: large leafy vegetable available in several different varieties.

Clockwise from top: Red cabbage, Chinese cabbage, savoy cabbage.

CARAMEL TOPPING: a caramel-flavoured syrup usually used in milk drinks or on ice-cream.

CHEESE:

Bocconcini: small balls of mild, delicate cheese packaged in water or whey to keep them white and soft. The water should be just milky and cheese should be white; yellowing indicates that it is stale.

Cheddar: we used a full-flavoured cheddar.

Cream cheese: also known as Philly.

Cottage: soft, unripened, mild-tasting curd cheese of different fat content from skim milk to full-cream milk.

Fresh goats' milk: we used a mild-flavoured goats' cheese.

Gruyere: a Swiss cheese with small holes and a nutty, slightly salty flavour.

Jarlsberg: a Norwegian cheese made from cows' milk; it has large holes and a mild nutty taste.

Kefalogravier: a semi-hard cheese with a smooth texture and a mild salty after-taste; made from sheep's milk.

Mozzarella: a fresh, semi-soft cheese with a delicate, clean, fresh curd taste; has a low melting point and stringy texture when heated.

Neufchatel: soft, unripened or fresh curd cheese. It resembles cream cheese but contains more moisture.

Parmesan: sharp-tasting cheese used as a flavour accent. We prefer to use fresh parmesan cheese, however, it is available already finely grated.

Pecorino: hard cheese, straw-coloured with grainy texture and sharp-tangy flavour.

Ricotta: a fresh, unripened, light curd cheese of rich flavour.

Tasty: use a firm good-tasting cheddar.

True blue: a smooth and creamy white-blue mould cheese.

CHILLIES: are available in many different types and sizes. The small ones (bird's eye or bird peppers) are the hottest. Use tight rubber gloves when chopping fresh chillies as they can burn your skin. The seeds are the hottest part of the chillies so remove them if you want to reduce the heat content of recipes.

Chilli powder: ground dried chillies.

Chilli sauce: we used a hot or sweet Chinese variety. It consists of chillies, salt and vinegar. We use it sparingly so that you can easily increase amounts in recipes to suit your taste.

Dried chilli flakes: are available at Asian food stores.

CHORIZO SAUSAGE: Spanish and Mexican highly spiced pork sausages seasoned with garlic, cayenne pepper, chilli, etc. They are ready to eat when bought. If unavailable, use a spicy salami. See picture with cabanossi.

CORIANDER: also known as cilantro and Chinese parsley, it is available fresh, ground and in seed form. The leaves, roots and stems can be used.

Clockwise from right: Coriander, ground coriander, flat-leafed parsley.

CORNFLOUR: cornstarch.

CREAM: is simply a light pouring cream, also known as half 'n' half.

Thickened (whipping): is specified when necessary in recipes.

Reduced: a canned product with 25 percent fat content.

Sour: a thick commercially cultured soured cream.

Sour light: a less dense commercially cultured soured cream; do not substitute this for sour cream.

CREME DE CACAO: chocolate-flavoured liqueur.

CURRY POWDER: a convenient combination of spices in powdered form. Curry powder consists of chilli, coriander, cumin, fennel, fenugreek and turmeric in varying proportions.

CUSTARD POWDER: pudding mix.

DUCK, CHINESE ROAST: available from Asian food stores.

DUCK LIVER PATE: use chicken liver pate if unavailable.

EGGPLANT: aubergine.

ENDIVE: a curly-leafed vegetable, mainly used in salads.

Endive.

FENNEL: vegetable with aniseed-tasting bulb and leaves; bulb can be eaten uncooked in salads or may be braised, steamed or stir-fried in savoury dishes. Leaves can be chopped and added to dishes.

FISH SAUCE: an essential ingredient in the cooking of a number of South East Asian countries, including Thailand and Vietnam. It is made from the liquid drained from salted, fermented anchovies. It has a very strong smell and taste. Use sparingly until you acquire the taste.

FIVE SPICE POWDER: a pungent mixture of ground spices which include cinnamon, cloves, fennel, star anise and Szechwan peppers.

FLOUR, PLAIN: all-purpose flour.

GARBANZOS: canned chick peas. They are a staple food in the Middle East; are available from supermarkets and health food shops.

GARAM MASALA: there are many variations of the combinations of cardamom, cinnamon, cloves, coriander, cumin and nutmeg used to make up this spice, used often in Indian cooking. Sometimes pepper is used to make a hot variation. Garam masala is readily available in jars.

GARLIC: strong-scented pungent bulb with a distinctive taste. A bulb consists of cloves; use number of cloves specified in individual recipes. See picture with red Spanish onions.

GHERKIN: cornichon.

GINGER:

Fresh, green or root: scrape away outside skin and grate, chop or slice ginger as required. Fresh, peeled ginger can be preserved with enough dry sherry to cover; keep in jar in refrigerator; it will keep for months.

Ground: is also available but should not be substituted for fresh ginger.

Fresh ginger.

GRAND MARNIER: an orange-flavoured liqueur. Cointreau can be substituted.

HERBS: we have specified when to use fresh or dried herbs. We used dried (not ground) herbs in the proportion of 1:4 for fresh herbs; for example, 1 teaspoon dried herbs instead of 4 teaspoons (1 tablespoon) chopped fresh herbs.

HOI SIN SAUCE: a thick, sweet Chinese barbecue sauce made from salted black beans, onions and garlic.

HORSERADISH CREAM: paste of horseradish, oil, mustard and flavourings.

JAM: conserve.

KAHLUA: a Mexican liqueur flavoured with coffee.

KIRSCH: a liqueur distilled from cherries.

KIWI FRUIT: Chinese gooseberries.

LASAGNE, INSTANT: these pasta sheets don't need to be pre-cooked; check packet directions; available from supermarkets.

LEMON GRASS: needs to be bruised or chopped before using. It will keep in a jug of water at room temperature for several weeks; the water must be changed daily. It can be bought dried. To reconstitute: place several pieces of dried lemon grass in a bowl; cover with hot water, stand 20 minutes; drain. This amount is a substitute for 1 stem of fresh lemon grass.

Lemon grass.

LOBSTER: crayfish.

MALIBU: tropical coconut drink flavoured with light Jamaican rum liqueur.

MARINARA MIX: a mixture of uncooked, chopped seafood usually including prawns,

mussels, fish and octopus or squid.

MARZIPAN: a paste made from marzipan meal.

MIRIN: a sweet rice wine used in Japanese cooking. Substitute 1 teaspoon sugar and 1 teaspoon dry sherry for each tablespoon of mirin, if preferred.

MIXED SPICE: a blend of ground spices usually consisting of cinnamon, allspice and nutmeg.

MUSHROOMS: We used fresh mushrooms, plus other different types of mushrooms in our recipes.

Clockwise from left: Oyster mushooms, shitake mushrooms, Chinese dried mushrooms.

MUSSEL MEAT: cooked mussels removed from the shell. See picture with scallops.

MUSTARD, SEEDED: a French style of mustard with crushed mustard seeds.

MUSTARD SEEDS: tiny seeds used in curries, pickling and making mustard; seeds can be black, (spicy and piquant), brown (less piquant) or white (milder).

NOODLES: See picture at right.

OIL: polyunsaturated vegetable oil.

Olive: we used a virgin olive oil but use the grade you prefer. Olive oil comes in several

different grades with each grade having a different flavour. The most flavoursome is the extra virgin variety usually used in homemade dressings. Extra virgin olive oil is the purest quality virgin oil. Virgin oil is obtained only from the pulp of high-grade fruit. Pure olive oil is pressed from the pulp and kernels of second grade olives. Extra light olive oil is lighter in colour and flavour to pure and virgin.

Sesame: made from roasted, crushed white sesame seeds. It is always used in small quantities. Do not use for frying.

ONION, RED SPANISH: red-skinned, pink-fleshed variety, almost odourless and popular in salads.

From left: Garlic, bulb and cloves, green shallots, red Spanish onion.

OYSTER SAUCE: a rich brown sauce made from oysters cooked in salt and soy sauce, then thickened with different types of starches.

PANCETTA: is Italian in origin; is a ready-to-eat processed meat made from pork belly which has been salted, cured and lightly spiced. See picture with pastrami.

Picture shows noodles used in this book: 1. Capellini egg noodles, 2. rice vermicelli, 3. dried egg noodles, 4. Japanese somen noodles, 5. fine fresh egg noodles, 6. fresh egg noodles, 7. gow gees pastry, 8. egg pastry sheets.

Picture shows some of the pastas used in this book: 1. capelli d'angelo pasta, 2. extra large pasta shells, 3. curled frilly pasta, 4. wholemeal pasta wheels, 5. conchigliette pasta, 6. linguine pasta, 7. vegeroni pasta spirals, 8. pasta crests.

PARSLEY, FLAT-LEAFED: popular herb also known as continental or Italian parsley. See picture with coriander.

PASTA: See picture below.

PASTA SAUCE: we used bottled products; one containing beef and one without meat. based on tomatoes; available from supermarkets.

PASTRAMI: highly seasoned smoked beef ready to eat when bought.

Clockwise from top: Prosciutto, pastrami, pancetta.

PASTRY, READY ROLLED PUFF: frozen sheets of puff pastry available from supermarkets.

PEAS:

Snow: also known as mange tout (eat all), sugar peas or Chinese peas.

Sugar snap: a young tender spring pea with edible pod.

PECANS: nuts of the hickory tree with a sweet, oily kernel; walnuts can be substituted.

PEPPERCORNS, GREEN: berries of the pepper plant; available in cans from supermarkets.

PEPPERS: capsicums or bell peppers.

From left: Red pepper, pimientos.

PEPPER, SEASONED: a combination of pepper, red pepper, garlic flakes, paprika and natural chicken extract.

PIMIENTOS (sweet red peppers): are preserved in brine in cans or jars. See picture with peppers.

PLUM SAUCE: a dipping sauce which consists of plums preserved in vinegar,

From left: Snow peas, sugar snap peas.

sweetened with sugar and flavoured with chillies and spices.

POLENTA: cornmeal.

PORK, BARBECUED RED: roasted pork fillets available from many Asian food and specialty stores.

PORT WINE JELLY: a port-flavoured jelly preserve; apple jelly can be substituted.

PRAWNS: also known as shrimp.

PROSCIUTTO: uncooked, unsmoked ham cured in salt, ready to eat when bought. See picture with pastrami.

RIND: zest.

RUM: we used a dark underproof rum.

SAFFRON: the most expensive of all spices, is available in threads or ground form. It is made from the dried stamens of the crocus flower.

SAKE: Japan's favourite rice wine; is used in cooking, marinading and as part of dipping sauces. If sake is unavailable, dry sherry, vermouth or brandy can be substituted.

SALMON, ATLANTIC: farmed variety of fish available all year.

SALMON ROE: caviar, eggs of salmon.

SAMBAL OELEK: a paste made from ground chillies and salt.

SCALLOPS: we used the scallops with coral (roe) attached; they require minimal preparation.

From top: Scallops, mussel meat.

SHALLOTS, GREEN: also known as spring onions and scallions. See picture with red Spanish onions.

SHRIMP PASTE: a powerful dark brown flavouring made from salted dried shrimp.

SOY SAUCE: made from fermented soya beans. The light sauce is generally used with white meat, the darker variety with red meat. There is a multi-purpose salt-reduced sauce available, also Japanese soy sauce. It is a matter of personal taste which sauce you use.

SPATCHCOCK: small chicken about 400g to 500g.

SPINACH (silverbeet): remove coarse white stems, cook green leafy parts as individual recipes indicate. See picture below.

From left: English spinach, silverbeet.

125

SPINACH, ENGLISH: a soft-leaved vegetable, more delicate in taste than silverbeet; however, young silverbeet can be substituted. See picture previous page.

STOCK CUBES: available in beef, chicken or vegetable flavours. Use 1 large crumbled stock cube to every 2 cups water. These cubes contain salt, so allow for this when seasoning food.

SUGAR:

Brown: soft, fine, brown sugar.

Castor: fine granulated table sugar.

Crystal: granulated table sugar.

Icing: confectioners' or powdered sugar.

Pure icing: pure powdered sugar without the addition of cornflour as in icing sugar mixture.

SULTANAS: seedless white raisins.

TERIYAKI MARINADE: a blend of soy sauce, wine, vinegar and spices.

TOAST BREAD: thick sliced white bread.

TOFU: made from boiled, crushed soy beans to give a type of milk, a coagulant is added, then the curds are drained and cotton tofu is the result; this is the ordinary firm tofu used in this book. Silken tofu is undrained and more fragile. Store tofu in the refrigerator covered with water, which must be changed daily.

TOMATO:

Paste: a concentrated tomato puree used in flavouring soups, stews, sauces, etc.

Puree: canned, pureed tomatoes (not tomato paste). Use fresh, peeled, pureed tomatoes as a substitute, if preferred.

Sauce: tomato ketchup.

Sun-dried: are dried tomatoes sometimes bottled in oil.

Supreme: a canned product consisting of tomatoes, onions, celery, peppers and seasonings.

TURKEY BREAST ROLL: ready-to-eat turkey available from delicatessens.

VECON: a natural vegetable stock paste available in health food stores.

VINEGAR: we used both white and brown (malt) vinegar in this book.

Balsamic: originated in the province of Modena, Italy. Regional wine is specially processed then aged in antique wooden casks to give pungent flavour.

Cider: vinegar made from fermented apples.

Red wine: made from red wine, often flavoured with herbs, spices, fruit, etc.

Rice: a colourless seasoned vinegar containing sugar and salt.

WASABI PASTE: a paste made from Japanese horseradish; available from Asian food stores.

WINE: we used good-quality dry white and red wines.

Green ginger: an Australian-made alcoholic sweet wine infused with finely ground ginger.

WONTON WRAPPERS: are thin squares or rounds of fresh noodle dough. Use egg pastry sheets if unavailable; available from Asian food stores.

WORCESTERSHIRE SAUCE: is a spicy sauce used mainly on red meat.

ZUCCHINI: courgette.

Index

FACTS AND FIGURES

Wherever you live, you'll be able to use our recipes with the help of these easy-to-follow conversions. While these conversions are approximate only, the difference between an exact and the approximate conversion of various liquid and dry measures is but minimal and will not affect your cooking results.

DRY MEASURES

Metric	Imperial
15g	1/2oz
30g	1oz
60g	2oz
90g	3oz
125g	4oz (1/4lb)
155g	5oz
185g	6oz
220g	7oz
250g	8oz (1/2lb)
280g	9oz
315g	10oz
345g	11oz
375g	12oz (3/4lb)
410g	13oz
440g	14oz
470g	15oz
500g	16oz (1lb)
750g	24oz (1 1/2lb)
1kg	32oz (2lb)

LIQUID MEASURES

Metric	Imperial
30ml	1 fluid oz
60ml	2 fluid oz
100ml	3 fluid oz
125ml	4 fluid oz
150ml	5 fluid oz (1/4 pint/1 gill)
190ml	6 fluid oz
250ml	8 fluid oz
300ml	10 fluid oz (1/2 pint)
500ml	16 fluid oz
600ml	20 fluid oz (1 pint)
1000ml (1 litre)	1 3/4 pints

HELPFUL MEASURES

Metric	Imperial
3mm	1/8in
6mm	1/4in
1cm	1/2in
2cm	3/4in
2.5cm	1in
5cm	2in
6cm	2 1/2in
8cm	3in
10cm	4in
13cm	5in
15cm	6in
18cm	7in
20cm	8in
23cm	9in
25cm	10in
28cm	11in
30cm	12in (1ft)

MEASURING EQUIPMENT

The difference between one country's measuring cups and another's is, at most, within a 2 or 3 teaspoon variance. (For the record, 1 Australian metric measuring cup holds approximately 250ml.) The most accurate way of measuring dry ingredients is to weigh them. When measuring liquids, use a clear glass or plastic jug with the metric markings.

Note: North America and UK use 15ml tablespoons. Australian tablespoons measure 20ml. All cup and spoon measurements are level.

How To Measure

When using graduated metric measuring cups, shake dry ingredients loosely into the appropriate cup. Do not tap the cup on a bench or tightly pack the ingredients unless directed to do so. Level top of measuring cups and measuring spoons with a knife. When measuring liquids, place a clear glass or plastic jug with metric markings on a flat surface to check accuracy at eye level.

We use large eggs having an average weight of 60g.

OVEN TEMPERATURES

These oven temperatures are only a guide. Always check the manufacturer's manual.

	C° (Celsius)	F° (Fahrenheit)	Gas Mark
Very slow	120	250	1
Slow	150	300	2
Moderately slow	160	325	3
Moderate	180 - 190	350 - 375	4
Moderately hot	200 - 210	400 - 425	5
Hot	220 - 230	450 - 475	6
Very hot	240 - 250	500 - 525	7